# THE DIVORCE ACT IN PRACTICE

GW00482900

UNITED KINGDOM
Sweet & Maxwell
London


AUSTRALIA
LBC Information Services
Sydney


CANADA AND USA
Carswell
Toronto • Ontario


NEW ZEALAND
Brooker's
Auckland


SINGAPORE AND MALAYSIA
Thomson Information (S.E. Asia)
Singapore

# THE DIVORCE ACT IN PRACTICE

*Editor*

GEOFFREY SHANNON
Solicitor

*Contributors*
Rosemary Horgan, Solicitor
Stephanie Coggans, Solicitor
Claire Archbold, Barrister and Lecturer in Law
Hilary Walpole, Tax Consultant
John D. McCarthy, Pensions Consultant

ROUND HALL LTD
1999

Published in 1999 by
Round Hall Ltd
Brehon House, 4 Upper Ormond Quay,
Dublin 7

Typeset by
Gough Typesetting Services
Dublin

Printed by
Genprint, Dublin


ISBN 1-85800-152-8

A catalogue record for this book
is available from the British Library.

# Table of Contents

# Foreword

## David Byrne SC

*Address by the then Attorney General and
now Ireland's Commissioner to the European Union,
DIT Conference on Divorce, Saturday, April 24,1999.*

It gives me great pleasure to open this conference organised by the
Department of Legal Studies here in DIT Aungier Street. I would
like to acknowledge at the outset Dr Ellen Hazelkorn, Director of the
Faculty of Applied Arts, and thank her for the invitation to address
you this morning. I would like to compliment other staff members
including Bruce Carolan and Geoffrey Shannon on the organisation
of today's discussions.

I have had an opportunity to look at some of the papers which
will be delivered over the course of the day. There is no doubt that
this is an interesting and thought provoking subject involving analysis of the operation of legislation which is relatively new in the general scheme of things – the Family Law (Divorce) Act 1996.

I believe that conferences such as this one perform a valuable
function in bringing together experts who can share their insight and
knowledge. The sharing of hands-on experience of the everyday working of legislation provides us with a useful audit of those legislative
provisions and their effectiveness in practical terms.

I believe that the outcome of discussions such as the one proposed for today can inform the legislative process whether in high-
lighting the need for reform or providing lessons for future legislative
initiatives.

It is important that channels of communication are opened and
maintained between the people who formulate policy and draft legislation and the organisations and individuals who must operate the
laws and work within them on a daily basis. We must also be careful
never to allow a situation to develop where legislation is formulated
and drafted at some remove from the reality of everyday experience

and practicalities. Initiatives such as this conference go some way towards ensuring that that does not occur.

The introduction of divorce marked a watershed in Irish legal and social history. It has also led to the introduction of a substantial and wide-ranging new body of law. Inevitably, when the legal landscape changes to this degree, there will be initial difficulties and uncertainties. It is important that this opportunity to highlight those – and maybe suggest solutions – is seized.

I am pleased to note the involvement of Ms Claire Archbold, a practitioner from Northern Ireland, in today's proceedings. Family law is an area where a comparative perspective is often extremely valuable, and what could be more instructive than to hear about experiences in the jurisdiction closest to our own.

The title of today's conference is "Divorce – A Clean Break with the Past?". I am aware that the maintenance regime introduced in the Family Law (Divorce) Act 1996, has been subject to academic criticism as not providing a "clean break", in financial terms, following divorce. In effect, the new divorce legislation has continued the old common law tradition of a life-long spousal support obligation, even where the spouses' marriage has been legally declared to be over and the parties free to remarry.

The "clean break" model for post-divorce maintenance involves an irrevocable final settlement with no continuing support for the former spouses. It is regarded as simple, clear and final.

I suppose it is fair to ask why the Oireachtas chose not to allow couples the option of a financial "clean break" on divorce. While it is not of course open to me to second guess or comment on the motives of the Oireachtas in this regard, it is worth considering the context in which the divorce legislation was introduced.

The Irish people ascribe a very high value to the institution of marriage. It emerged very clearly during the pre-referendum debate that the electorate had a strong concern for the position of the financially weaker party to the marriage. I think it is fair to say that generally the Irish people, although in favour of the introduction of divorce, did not regard divorce as being an easy solution to the problem of marital breakdown. They do not see it as being a neat, clean or pain-free process and recognise that it will have enduring consequences.

While the "clean break" option does have the advantages of being simple, clear and final as I mentioned, it does have a number of serious downsides. It has been found to contribute to an increase in poverty among women. It could be said that it is in fact only useful for couples who have assets which may be sold and divided, for those couples where both parties are economically active outside the home, for those couples who are on an equal footing in terms of bargaining power, and – in particular – for those couples who do not have children.

It has been shown to impact with particular unfairness on marriages where the woman entered the marriage in the expectation that her contribution to the family enterprise would be made within the home, and that in return, she could expect life-long material support from her husband.

It seems to me that these concerns were at the forefront of the debate on divorce in advance of the referendum. The Irish electorate ultimately chose – by a tiny majority – to opt for the introduction of divorce in this jurisdiction. This realistic response to the demand for the introduction of divorce was, I believe, tempered by a very real concern on the part of the electorate for the position of women and children in divorce.

It is this compassionate consideration for the vulnerable parties to divorce that, in my view, led the Oireachtas to conclude that once-off final settlements in the area of divorce would not be acceptable to the Irish people and therefore should not, for now, be an option.

That is just one perspective on this debate and I look forward to hearing the outcome of your discussions today. I wish you every success with the day's proceedings. I also wish to thank Dr Ellen Hazelkorn once again for her kind invitation and I declare the conference officially open.

*David Byrne*
*April 1999*

# Preface

## *Geoffrey Shannon, Solicitor*

This book arises from a conference held by the Department of Legal studies at the Dublin Institute of Technology on April 24, 1999. The proceedings addressed the absence of a "clean break" doctrine in Irish divorce law, and speakers considered the wisdom of this lacuna. An array of excellent speakers presented papers that provided an overview of divorce legislation in Northern and Southern Ireland. Attorney General David Byrne (now Ireland's Commissioner to the European Union) opened the proceedings with some thought provoking comments. Thus, the conference began with and was informed by a healthy, creative tension. A large number of delegates attended the proceedings and participated in a sometimes heated discussion.

This book assesses the impact of divorce in Ireland two years after its inception. It carries a number of well analysed papers on various aspects of divorce from practice and procedure to a view of divorce from the North. For the practitioner and academic the book gives a compendium of information and background which, gathered together in one place, gives an understanding of the area which it is hoped will supplement the range of sources currently available.

Before discussing the contents of the book, it might be useful to give some idea of the background to the development of divorce law in Ireland. From the 1980s onwards, pressure mounted for the introduction of divorce in Ireland. The right to end an unhappy marriage and marry again was increasingly perceived as a fundamental right that should be available to all. By early 1990 the absence of divorce was seen as insensitive to the process of marital breakdown, anachronistic and hypocritical. On November 24, 1995 the Irish people, by the slimmest of a majority, voted to remove the absolute Constitutional ban on the dissolution of marriage.

The new Article 41.3.2° was incorporated into the Constitution on June 17, 1996 upon the Fifteenth Amendment to the Constitution Bill being signed by the President. This Article now provides that a court designated by law may grant a dissolution of marriage where, but only where, it is satisfied that:

> "i.   at the date of the institution of the proceedings, the spouses have lived apart from one another for a period of, or periods amounting to, at least four years during the previous five years,
>
> ii.   there is no reasonable prospect of a reconciliation between the spouses,
>
> iii.  such provision as the court considers proper having regard to the circumstances exists or will be made for the spouses, any children of either or both of them and any other person prescribed by law, and
>
> iv.   any further conditions prescribed by law are complied with."

The provisions of the new Article 41.3.2° have been put into effect by the Family Law (Divorce) Act 1996 which became law on February 27, 1997. With the Family Law (Divorce) Act 1996 Ireland adopted a no-fault divorce system. The scheme of divorce entered into continues the old common-law tradition of a life-long spousal support obligation. This acknowledgement that marriage may create permanent support obligations can be viewed as incompatible with the "clean break" doctrine. The papers published in this book review the foregoing proposition in the context of financial provision on divorce.

The Family Law (Divorce) Act 1996 is closely modelled on the Judicial Separation and Family Law Reform Act 1989 as amended by the Family Law Act 1995. In fact, the basis and criteria for awards of maintenance on divorce contained in the 1996 Act merely replicates those contained in the 1995 Act. Significantly, section 22 of the Family Law (Divorce) Act 1996 provides for orders, including maintenance orders, to be varied or discharged if there is a change in circumstances or new evidence. Under the terms of section 22, the court may vary or discharge the following orders:

1.   maintenance pending suit orders (section 12);

2.   periodical payments, secured periodical payments and lump sum orders (section 13);

3.   property adjustment orders under section 14(1)(b),(c) or (d);

4.   an order under section 15(1)(a);

5.   a financial compensation order (section 16); and

6.   a pension adjustment order (section 17(2) – "retirement benefits").

This section, Stephanie Coggans argues in Chapter 2, clearly prevents any "clean break" settlement. The Family Law (Divorce) Act 1996 in its ancillary relief orders also provides that spouses and ex-spouses can seek ancillary relief. Consequently, support obligations after divorce continue for the lifetime of the spouses, save in certain very limited circumstances. This book seeks to address *inter alia* the circumstances in which support obligations continue under the terms of the divorce legislation.

   The papers included in this book review the judicial approach to certainty in the law of financial provision on divorce. McGuinness J. in the High Court in *J.D. v. D.D.*, considering a claim for a lump sum payment in return for a "clean break" in a judicial separation case, concluded that a "clean break" was not a statutory option even where the parties wanted one. According to McGuinness J:

> "the Oireachtas has made it clear that a 'clean break' situation is not to be sought and that, if anything, financial finality is virtually to be prevented."[1]

The Supreme Court, however, in *P. O'D. v. A. O'D.* has expressed the desire for finality in family law.[2] Given the range of judicial views on the treatment of "final" settlement agreements, clarification of the matter is urgently needed. In the end, I believe the balance should tilt towards fairness rather than finality. I hope this book will assist in facilitating debate on the competing objectives identified.

   Finally, I would like to outline briefly the contents of the individual chapters. Commissioner Byrne in his foreword outlines the Government's position with respect to the absence of a "clean break" option.

   In Chapter 1, Rosemary Horgan explores and analyses divorce in Ireland since its inception, considering the evolution of divorce in Ireland and how the Family Law (Divorce) Act 1996 has worked in practice.

   In Chapter 2, Stephanie Coggans examines how the maintenance and property provisions of the divorce legislation operate and considers the importance of discovery when applying for a divorce decree.

---

[1]   [1997] 3 I.R. 89.
[2]   [1998] 1 I.L.R.M. 543.

In Chapter 3, Claire Archbold provides a view from the North – "the part of Ireland which has longer term experience of divorce law in practice". She reviews, *inter alia*, the "clean break" basis of ancillary relief orders in the North, as compared to the "sufficient provision" basis in this jurisdiction.

In Chapter 4, Hilary Walpole examines how divorce affects the tax situation of the parties. It is worth noting that there has been comparatively little research into whether the tax system affects marital behaviour. In the USA, the erosion of a previous generous tax subsidy has led commentators to claim that a couple would be more secure financially getting divorced than staying married, and that working married couples with children are penalised. Whittington and Alm suggest that the taxation system in the USA acts as an incentive to divorce, although they acknowledge the effect as being "very modest".[3]

In Chapter 5, John McCarthy reviews how the all important pension adjustment order has been applied. This paper did not form part of the initial conference series. However, given the complexity and importance of this provision, I believe that any review of the divorce jurisdiction would be incomplete without analysis of this order.

In conclusion, the task of publishing this book was made easier by the co-operation received from the expert contributors. I would like to express my deepest thanks and appreciation to them. Professor David Gwynn Morgan of University College Cork initially proposed the idea for a conference on divorce. He suggested this to Bruce Carolan at the annual meeting of the Advisory Committee on Legal Education and Training. I thank him for this suggestion. I also wish to thank and acknowledge the assistance of Catherine Dolan of Round Hall Ltd and Bruce Carolan of the Dublin Institute of Technology.

I hope you enjoy this collection of essays, and invite interested parties to contact Bruce Carolan, Head of Legal Studies, at the Dublin Institute of Technology with ideas for similar conferences in the future.

*Geoffrey Shannon,*
*Solicitor, Lecturer in Law,*
*Department of Legal Studies,*
*Dublin Institute of Technology.*
*November 1999*

---

[3]  Whittington and Alm, "Til Death or Taxes Do Us Part: The Effect of Income Taxation on Divorce" (1997) *Journal of Human Resources* 322 at 388–412.

# Table of Cases

# Table of Legislation

## IRELAND

### Constitution of Ireland 1937

### Statutes

**Statutory Instruments**

**Rules of Court**

# NORTHERN IRELAND

# ENGLAND

# SCOTLAND

# Chapter 1

# Divorce – The Irish Experience

## *Rosemary Horgan**

## BACKGROUND

The total ban on divorce contained in the original Article 41.3.2° of the 1937 Irish Constitution resulted in the complete absence of a divorce jurisdiction in Ireland until 1996. Unhappily, this did not result in the absence of marriage breakdown in Ireland. While other jurisdictions wrestled with the possibility of introducing "compulsory mediation" for divorcing couples, until 1989 we in Ireland had no legislative infrastructure facilitating legal separation on a humane basis. The action for *divorce a mensa et thoro* was limited to the fault grounds of adultery, cruelty and unnatural practices. It did not come in a "package" coupled with ancillary reliefs which were consequent upon separation. The general principal of separate property meant that anything owned by a spouse prior to the marriage continued to belong to them after the ceremony. Spouses, and in particular wives who availed of it, had to establish a legal entitlement to an interest in the family home, or other property. In a society where the husband was, in most cases, the sole earner and the wife remained in the family home raising the children and possibly doing some part-time work, unravelling the domestic arrangements to establish an equitable interest in property was not an easy one. One had to establish a "bricks and mortar" interest as opposed to an emotional attachment by virtue of time spent cooking/ cleaning/decorating/gardening and the like.

The courts were scrupulous in ensuring both an entitlement to the decree itself and any entitlement under the Married Women's Status Act 1957. The issue to be determined was "whose is this" and not "to whom shall this be given".[1] Neither could the Constitution which

---

*Rosemary Horgan BCL, LL.B, LL.M, Solicitor is head of the family law department, Ronan Daly Jermyn, Solicitors, Cork. She is Chairman of the Law Society of Ireland's Family Law and Civil Legal Aid Committee.

upheld and promoted the family based on marriage, ameliorate the
position of property rights on separation. Neither Article 41.1.1° nor
Article 41.1.2° was held to create or bestow any particular right within
the family whether to property or otherwise.[2] Against this background
many couples separated informally or by deed of separation on marriage breakdown. The expression "grass widow/ widower" discreetly
conveyed the status of such a person in the country.

The only way to end the marriage was through the process of
obtaining a decree of nullity of marriage. Over time it became easier
for the camel to pass through the eye of the "nullity needle". The
complexity of the nature of this remedy is beyond the scope of this
chapter, however, there is no doubt that it became more judicially
developed in the absence of a divorce jurisdiction. With the advent of
civil legal aid the High Court became more accessible to litigants
wishing to pursue the nullity remedy. The draconian legal consequences attaching to nullity, including the high burden of proof, and
the length of such proceedings made this option attractive mainly to
those wishing to remarry. Nullity still has very stark and indeed sometimes unfair consequences for the dependent party to the marriage,
particularly if the "marriage" subsisted for many years until declared
null and void or void *ab initio*. Curiously this harsh position is also
supportable because of the treasured position of marriage under the
Constitution.

Irish people took a resourceful and practical approach. Catholic
Church annulments were frequently obtained so as to facilitate a second religious marriage ceremony. Although of no legal effect, this
satisfied the social propriety of some people. Similarly many people
resident in Ireland obtained foreign divorces which would not be recognised in Ireland as valid, but similarly satisfied social propriety.
The practice was so common that the Revenue Commissioners by
concession, for income tax and capital gains tax purposes treated
couples who had gone through a second marriage as "married" even
though it appeared that the second marriage was not legally valid and
was in fact bigamous. The Domicile and Recognition of Foreign Divorces Act 1986 abolished the dependent domicile of wives and provided for recognition of a divorce granted in a country where either
spouse was domiciled at the date of the institution of the divorce

---

[1]   *Pettit v. Pettit* [1970] A.C 777.
[2]   *Murray v. Ireland* [1985] I.R. 532 and *L. v. L* [1992] 2 I.R. 77 (Sup. Ct.).

proceedings. Prior to that the rule was that both spouses had to be domiciled in the country where the decree was granted. Subsequent case law has confirmed, however, that regardless of when made, a foreign decree will be recognised if at the date of the institution of the proceedings either spouse was domiciled within the jurisdiction of the foreign court.[3] The extension of the recognition principles once again to encompass situations where the petitioner was ordinarily resident rather than domiciled in the foreign jurisdiction has been recommended so as to avoid "limping marriages", that is marriages recognised as dissolved in the country which granted the divorce but deemed valid and subsisting marriages in Ireland.[4] The recent High Court judgment of McGuinness J. extends the common law rule for recognition of foreign divorces to ordinary residence which is the same basis upon which Irish legislation gives jurisdiction to Irish courts to grant divorces.[5] In fact, the forthcoming Brussels II Regulation will further assist in the recognition of foreign divorces in Ireland and will alleviate many problems currently encountered by foreign divorcees.

## Domestic Violence

The background of domestic violence in marriage breakdown has been subliminal. Legislative civil relief for domestic violence has been available since 1976.[6] The legislation was designed to produce a "short sharp shock" for the perpetrator of domestic violence. The remedy of "barring order" was improved and strengthened over the years.[7] The tendency for repeat applications however was very well known to those working at the coal face of this area of law. Although the law proclaimed that the legislation was not to be used as a remedy for marriage breakdown, this was in reality how many people achieved a separation. Fahey and Lyons' sociological study in 1995 showed

---

[3] *W. v. W* [1993] 2 I.R. 476; *Clancy v. Minister for Social Welfare*, unreported, High Court, February, 1994, *Lambert v. An tArd Chlaraitheoir* [1995] 2 I.R. 372 (High Court), and *VMcC v. JMcC* [1996] 2 Fam. L.J. 68.

[4] Shatter, *Family Law* (4th ed., 1997, Butterworths), p.421.

[5] *G.McG. v. D.W; A.R.* (notice party), unreported, High Court, McGuinness J, January 14, 1999 , see (1999) 1 I.J.F.L at 26–28.

[6] Family Law (Maintenance of Spouses and Children) Act 1976, s. 22.

[7] Family Law (Protection of Spouses and Children) Act 1981 and Domestic Violence Act 1996.

the reality of the two tiers operating within the family law system.[8] Family law books and indeed lawyers tend to look at different categories of legal remedies in a very compartmentalised manner. Consumers of legal services however take a more "needs" based approach.

The District Family Court is accessible to practically all litigants whether they are legally represented or not. Many people apply for protection but subsequently decide not to proceed with the barring application. Those practising in the area will be well used to this phenomonen in the area of domestic violence. One questions however whether the significant gap between the numbers of protection orders granted as opposed to the number of barring orders would be different if more litigants were legally represented. The benefit of legal representation is not available to everyone. The availability of legal aid is a most important factor in that equation.

## Judicial Separation

Notwithstanding the increase in marital breakdown, reform in the area of judicial separation was only introduced after the first failed referendum to change Article 41.3.2° and remove the total prohibition on divorce.[9] With hindsight it was curious that efforts would be made to provide a divorce jurisdiction in the complete absence of a realistic infrastructure for judicial separation. It would be very wrong to suggest that the Referendum was introduced without debate and analysis of "family policy" issues.[10] The debate which preceded the first divorce referendum was divisive but also showed the real fears of people about the consequences of divorce both in personal terms and for society as a whole. Separated people themselves were afraid of losing their Deserted Wives Allowance/Benefit and other social

---

[8]  Fahey and Lyons, *Marital Breakdown and Family Law in Ireland: A Sociological Study* (Oak Tree Press, 1995).

[9]  The Tenth Amendment of the Constitution, June 26, 1986 was rejected by 63.50% of those who voted.

[10]  See LRC Report on *Divorce a Mensa et Thoro* and Related Matters (LRC 8–1983), Joint Oireachtas Committee on Marriage Breakdown 1983, Social Reform of Marriage in Ireland, by Divorce Action Group November 1983, Dáil and Seanad Debates, Duncan, "The case for Divorce in The Irish Republic" (ICCL Report No.5 1982), Binchy, "Is Divorce the Answer?" (Irish Academic Press 1984) and numerous articles in the press in the period leading to the Referendum.

welfare entitlements consequent on marriage. The "clean break" culture in the English divorce jurisdiction lead to the fear that divorce would further impoverish separated wives. Farmers and business owners were afraid of the division of the farm or business on divorce. The perceived reality gap was far too wide for the ordinary voter to leap over.

The Judicial Separation and Family Law Reform Act 1989 was a radical departure from the earlier legislative provision. It introduced new grounds and procedures for obtaining a judicial separation, providing for the first time three "no fault grounds" in addition to three "fault grounds". It also provided an array of ancillary orders which could be made, at the discretion of the court on judicial separation. The availability of the very extensive range of financial and property orders under Part II of the Act made the legislation immediately attractive. Although this Act made no alteration in the ownership of the property of the spouses or children during the currency of the marriage it authorised the courts to make the following orders following a decree of judicial separation:

- A property adjustment order under section 15, under which the courts could order the transfer of property (any property not just the family home) between spouses or on behalf of a dependent child, or order that property be settled, or order that property already settled by marriage settlement be varied on behalf of one of the spouses or on behalf of a dependent child.

- An order granting sole rights of occupancy to one spouse and for the exclusion of the other spouse, or for the sale of the family home, dealing with the ownership or protection of property, or making a barring order under section 16.

- An order extinguishing succession rights under section 17.

- An order directing the sale of property to secure the payment of a periodical payments order, a lump sum order or a property adjustment order under section 18.

The existence of these powers which were available to the court having regard to the list of criteria set out in section 20, meant that many more cases were settled in addition to the cases actually heard and determined by the court. The property adjustment order was available on one occasion only and so practitioners could advise on settlement with some degree of certainty. Most settlements contained a

Property Adjustment Order of some sort in order to remove that particular Sword of Damocles.

The introduction of legislation designed to give each spouse equal rights in ownership to the family home and contents failed. The Bill also proposed to introduce matrimonial property and maintenance relief on the granting of a decree of nullity. *In Re The Matrimonial Home Bill 1993*[11] the Supreme Court held that such a provision providing for automatic joint ownership of all matrimonial homes would be repugnant to Article 41 of the Constitution in that it would be repugnant to the "authority of the family".[12] There was to be no future "community of property" provision on marriage in Ireland.

On a practical level however, marriage breakdown was being dealt with by the court through the 1989 Act and the ancillary relief provisions contained in it, and separation agreements were being concluded having regard to the powers available to the court under that legislation.

The Family Law Act 1995 amended the Judicial Separation and Family Law Reform Act, 1989 by repealing Part II of the 1989 Act in its entirety and replacing it with a new Part II of the 1995 Act which provided enhanced ancillary relief. It then became possible to obtain:

• A Pension Adjustment Order,

• A Pension Preservation Order, and

• A Financial Compensation Order.

The Pension Adjustment Order was also altered in that it was no longer confined to being obtained on one occasion only.

The Social Welfare (Consolidation) Act 1993, section 285 established the liability of spouses and parents to maintain their spouse and any dependent child, and section 286 (1) established the liability of a spouse or parent to contribute to the Department towards any benefit or allowance being paid to his/her spouse by the State. The Social Welfare code struggled to escape the anomaly of the Deserted Wives Benefit and provide a social welfare entitlement to all spouses who needed support regardless of the circumstances in which the spouse found themselves alone and raising dependent children. Sec-

---

[11] [1994] 1 I.R. 305.
[12] See Finlay C.J at 325.

tion 286 empowered the Department or a Health Board to apply to the District Court for an order directing that contributions be made. Section 298 established the liability of a recipient of a benefit or allowance to transfer maintenance payments made in compliance with an order of the Courts under the family legislation, to the Department of Social Welfare or Health Board. Failure to do so could result in the loss of the benefit or allowance. The establishment of the Maintenance Recovery Section of the Department to enforce these provisions was a very quiet affair however in contrast to the establishment of the controversial Child Support Agency in the United Kingdom.

The Family Law and Social Welfare (No. 2) Act 1995 also provided protection for the social welfare entitlements of validly divorced spouses who did not remarry. The second Divorce Referendum on November 24, 1995 was successful and passed into Irish law by 50.28 per cent of those who voted.

No constructive debate took place in advance of the Referendum on issues such as what precisely were to be the rights of "former spouses". How would the rights to maintenance of both the current and the former spouse be balanced. In fact, every effort was made to smooth over such issues by the bland assertion that there would be no loss of maintenance rights after divorce. In effect a type of serial monogamy with maintenance obligations more appropriate to polygamy where the financial obligations of marriage survived its demise. The experiences of the U.K jurisdiction as outlined in the Law Commission discussion paper entitled *The Financial Consequences of Divorce: The Basic Policy (1980)* dealing with the various models of financial provision subsequent to divorce and *The Scottish Law Commission in Ailment and Financial Provision (1981)* which pointed up the need for a balance between principle and discretion, was tacitly avoided by the pro divorce lobby.

There appeared to be a general anxiety to ensure that a divorce jurisdiction existed and postpone resolving other problems consequent on same. As has been pointed out however, this has resulted in the introduction of divorce without any reassessment of the basis on which maintenance is paid to former spouses.[13]

---

[13] Power, "Maintenance : No clean break with the past" (1998) 1 I.J.F.L at 15–19.

## GROUNDS FOR DIVORCE

The amended Article 41.3.2° provided that:

> A court designated by law may grant a dissolution of marriage, where but only where, it is satisfied that:

    i.   at the date of the institution of the proceedings, the spouses have lived apart from one another for a period of, or periods amounting to , at least four years during the previous five years,

    ii.  there is no reasonable prospect of reconciliation between the spouses,

    iii. such provision as the court considers proper having regard to the circumstances exists or will be made for the spouses, any children of either or both of them and any other person prescribed by law, and

    iv.  any further conditions prescribed by law are complied with.

The operative date for the constitutional amendment was June 19, 1996 and the first divorce case, *R.C v. C.C* [14] was based on the provisions of this constitutional amendment rather than on the legislative provisions of the Family Law (Divorce) Act 1996. Section 5 of the 1996 Act provides—

    (1)  Subject to the provisions of this Act, where, on application to it in that behalf by either of the spouses concerned, the court is satisfied that:

        (a)  at the date of the institution of the proceedings, the spouses have lived apart from one another for a period of, or periods amounting to, at least four years during the previous five years,

        (b)  there is no reasonable prospect of a reconciliation between the spouses, and

        (c)  such provision as the court considers proper having regard to the circumstances exists or will be made for the spouses and any dependent members of the family,

the court may, in exercise of the jurisdiction conferred by Article 41.3.2° of the Constitution grant a decree of divorce in respect of the marriage concerned.

    (2)  Upon the grant of the decree of the divorce, the court may, where appropriate, give such directions under section 11 of the [Guardi-

---

[14] [1997] 1 I.L.R.M. 401 and (1997) 1 F.L.R. 1.

anship of Infants] Act of 1964 as it considers proper regarding
the welfare (within the meaning of that Act), custody of, or right
of access to, any dependent member of the family concerned who
is an infant ( within the meaning of that Act) as if an application
had been made to it in that behalf under that section.[15]

## "Living Apart"

The chapter will only deal with the "four years living apart" requirement. The Act is designed so as not to inhibit attempts at reconciliation. The periods of cohabitation must not amount in aggregate to
more than one year within the five year period. " Living Apart" is not
defined by the 1996 legislation. Living apart is, however, also a requirement of grounds 2 (1)(d) and (e) of the 1989 Act and this Act
does provide that spouses shall be treated as living apart from each
other unless they are living with each other in the same household.
The standard of proof under the 1989 Act is declared to be "on the
balance of probabilities" while the 1996 Act is silent with regard to
the standard to be applied by the Court. Given the nature of the constitutional amendment however it seems likely that a higher level than
the civil standard would be applied in a contested case, as in the case
of the burden of proof in nullity cases.[16] The question arises as to
whether couples can be "living apart" although living under the one
roof. The answer to this question will depend upon the facts of the
individual case: are the parties living separate lives although under
the one roof? It is suggested that the case law in the U.K and New
Zealand is relevant though not determinative of the issue.

The case of *Fuller(ors Penfold) v. Fuller*[17] involved an altruistic
estranged wife who took in her seriously ill husband to care for him.
Although the wife provided her husband with food and did his laundry she was held by the Court of Appeal not to be living in the one
household with him "as husband and wife". Other cases of interest
are *Smith v. Smith*,[18] *Naylor v. Naylor*[19] *Hopes v. Hopes*[20] and *Le*

---

[15] The operative date of this section was February 27, 1997.
[16] In nullity cases, the petitioner must establish the case to a high degree of
    probability. See *E.C ( otherwise M) v. A.M* (1991) 10 Fam L.J .
[17] [1973] 2 All E.R. 650.
[18] 1939] 4 All E.R. 533.
[19] [1961] All E.R. 129.
[20] [1949] P 227 and 236.

*Brocq v. Le Brocq.*[21] There must be a separation of households as opposed to a mere separation of houses, the factum of desertion is present where one of the parties lives a completely separate life although under the one roof. *Mouncer v. Mouncer*[22] is instructive in this regard and concerns the case of an estranged couple who continued to reside in the one household to facilitate the husband having a continuing relationship with his children. This necessitated shared "family meals" although the couple slept in separate rooms. They were deemed to be living as "one household" and not living apart.

*Santos v. Santos*[23] referred to the necessity for a mental element to living apart, providing that more than physical separation was required. The parties would not be living apart where both parties recognised the marriage as subsisting. In this case the Court of Appeal held that living apart only commences when one party recognises that the marriage has come to an end.

There is a stream of authority on analogous Australian, New Zealand, United States and Canadian living apart provisions running in favour of mere physical separation *not* constituting "living apart".[24]

One can also have regard to the tax cases on the topic, for example *Eadie v. CIR,*[25] *D Ua Clothasaigh v. Patrick Mc Cartan,*[26] *Donovan v. Crofts*[27] and the recent UK tax case of *Holmes v. Mitchell*[28] arising out of which the U.K. revenue guidelines ask practical questions to determine the issue such as, is the house divided up between the couple and what are the arrangements for sharing common bathroom and kitchen facilities? How co-operative are the spouses with each other in ordinary household tasks, what are the financial arrangements between them, and how do they manage to avoid each other?[29]

It is suggested that the court would look at all these relevant is-

---

[21] [1964] 1 A.L.R 1085.

[22] [1972] 1 All E.R. 289.

[23] [1972] 2 All E.R. 246.

[24] See Cretney, *Principles of Family Law* (6th ed., 1997, Sweet & Maxwell), *Mc Rostie v. Mc Rostie* [1955] N.Z.L.R. 631; *Sullivan v Sullivan* [1958] N.Z.L.R. 912 and *Joe v. Joe* [1985] 3 N.Z.F.L.R. 675.

[25] 9 T.C 1

[26] I.T.C., Vol.2, 237.

[27] I.T.C., Vol.1, 126 and 129.

[28] [1991] S.T.C 25

[29] See Walpole, "Tax Implications of Divorce" (1999) 1 I.J.F.L 2. See also Chapter 4.

sues very closely if called upon to determine whether in fact the parties were living apart for the requisite period. The onus would be on the applicant to establish the case and the Court would scrutinise the facts carefully to discharge its constitutional obligation under Article 41.

## THE FACTUAL CONTEXT

When interpreting the following statistics, it is important to bear in mind that there is a level of carry over of applications/orders from one year to another. In addition, it is well to remember that trends and graphs are not always what they seem. The Department of Justice Equality and Law Reform produce their annual statistics for a period which effectively straddles two years, *e.g.* August 1, 1995 to 31 July 1996.[30] It is important therefore to bear in mind the date the relevant legislation came into operation. The Judicial Separation and Family Law Reform Act 1989 came into operation on April 19, 1989. The Family Law Act 1995 came into operation on October 2, 1995 and the Family Law (Divorce)Act came into operation at the end of February 1997.

The requirement to be separated for four years out of the previous five years before being entitled to seek a divorce ensures that many people will continue to seek a legal separation either by mutual agreement or through the court process. Most of the ancillary relief orders available on divorce are also available on separation and so a decree of judicial separation can act as a half-way house, severing the cohabitation requirement of marriage and setting in place financial arrangements consequent on separation but without actually ending the marriage. Available statistics show that most applications for judicial separation go to the Circuit Court rather than the High Court.

---

[30] In addition it should be said that the information and graphs generated from same were furnished by the Courts Division of the Department to the writer by fax on April 16, 1999, however figures supplied by the Courts Division on Sept. 23, 1999 differ slightly from the figures released in April. It would appear that different court areas collate information in different ways and there would appear to be an urgent need to review the method of collation, and nature of collation of statistical material.

### Judicial Separations 1995-1998

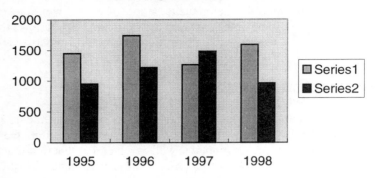

Series 1:  represents applications for judicial separation.
Series 2:  represents the numbers of orders made.

For the year ended July 31, 1995, there were 1,446 applications for judicial separation received and 951 orders granted. Of these, 1,398 were in the Circuit Court with only 48 in the High Court. For the year ended July 31, 1996 there were 1,739 judicial separation applications (1,670 at Circuit Court level and 69 at High Court level) and 1,213 granted (1,185 at Circuit level and 28 at High Court level). For the year ended July 31, 1997 the figures were 1,262 applications (1,208 at Circuit Court level and 54 at High Court level) and 1,481 orders (1,431 at Circuit Court level and 50 at High Court level). For the year ended July 31, 1998 the figures were 1,587 Applications (1531 at Circuit level and 56 at High Court level) and 961 orders granted (935 at Circuit Court level and 26 at High Court level ). It is therefore fair to say that there is a trend towards greater application at Circuit Court level rather than at High Court level. Tentative figures released by the Department for the period August 1, 1998 to December 31, 1998 and January 1, 1999 to January 31, 1999 show that so far there have been 956 applications for judicial separation received at Circuit Court level, and 534 decrees of judicial separation made at Circuit Court level. As the statistical year does not end until July 31, 1999 all that can be said is that the level of application at Circuit Court level is likely to be maintained in 1999.

Unfortunately the statistics do not tell us what percentage of applications were brought by wives or by husbands. Nor do the statistics enlighten us about the age groups of the litigants, their social class, whether they had children etc., and so analysis such as that undertaken by John Haskey in the United Kingdom on divorce is not possible.[31] Statistics are available for the "ancillary relief orders" made consequent upon separation and divorce however.

## Nullity Applications and decrees

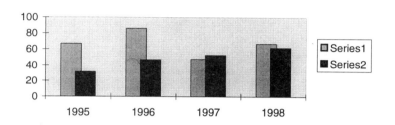

Series 1: represents nullity applications.
Series 2: represents decrees of nullity.

## NULLITY APPLICATIONS AND DECREES 1995–1998

The number of nullity applications declined in the period ended July 31, 1997, and increased again in the period ended July 31, 1998. It is far too early to say whether the introduction of divorce will dramatically affect the nullity jurisdiction. It is quite clear that the development of the nullity jurisdiction was achieved in the total absence of a divorce jurisdiction. Divorce can now be granted instead of a decree of nullity and possibly with fairer consequences.[32] Indeed nullity of

---

[31] Haskey, "The Proportion of Marriages ending in Divorce" (1982) 27 *Population Trends* 4, "Social Class and Socio-economic Differentials in Divorce in England and Wales" (1984) *Population Studies* 38, "Grounds for Divorce in England and Wales – A Social and Demographic Analysis" (1986) 18 J. Biosoc. Sci.,p. 127, Fig.2, Table 3, "Recent Trends in Divorce in England and Wales, the Effects of Legislative Changes" (1986) 44 *Population Trends*, p.11, figure 6 (at p.17), "Regional Patterns of Divorce in England and Wales" ( 1988) 52 *Population Trends* p.5, table 6 ( at p.13), "Children in Families Broken by Divorce" (1990) 61 *Population Trends*, p.34, figure 1(p.35), table 1 ( p.35).

[32] See Woods, "Nullity and Divorce – The New Alternatives?" (1999) 2 I.J.F.L at 12–18, where it is cogently argued that " It may not be unreasonable to presume that some of the apparent developments in the doctrine of nullity have been due, not so much to any obvious *lacuna* in the law, but to the particular circumstances of an especially deserving case."

marriage is now the only way of ending a marriage and at the same time closing off all financial obligations to the other partner. In the year ended July 31, 1995 and July 31, 1996 all applications were at High Court level, however with the advent of the Family Law Act 1995 the switch to commencement at Circuit Court level became immediately apparent. In the year ended July 31, 1997, with 28 Applications received in the Circuit Family Court and 20 applications received in the High Court in the former period, and 55 applications received in the Circuit Court and only 12 in the High Court in the latter period. Again, tentative figures released by the Department for the period August 1, 1998 to December 31, 1998, and January 1, 1999 to January 31, 1999 show that so far there have been 55 applications for nullity received at Circuit Court level and 27 decrees of nullity made. As the statistical year does not end until July 31, 1999 all that can be said is that the level of application for nullity at Circuit Court level is likely to show an increase in 1999 when firm figures are eventually released.

### Divorce Applications and Decrees

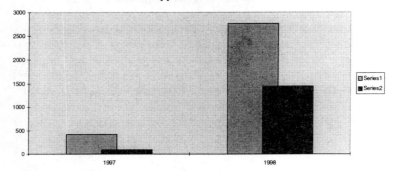

Series 1: represents applications for divorce.
Series 2: represents decrees of divorce.

## DIVORCE APPLICATIONS AND DECREES 1997 AND 1998

Many observers were surprised by the slow take up in the divorce jurisdiction after so many years lobbying for its introduction. It is suggested however that a variety of factors can be taken into account in this regard:

• Practitioners adopted a "wait and see" approach until some guidance emerged on the issue of finality, certainty and "clean break". Practitioners found it hard to reconcile the desirability for certainty and finality referred to in *F. v. F.*[33] with the clear legislative intention of an open ended entitlement to apply for financial relief following separation and divorce. McGuinness J. in *J.D. v D.D.*[34] confirmed the inability of the Court to apply a "clean break" even where the parties wanted one, and the facts of the case warranted one. In an *ex tempore* judgment of McGuinness J. in the case of *E.P. v. C.P.*[35] she also noted the desirability to have an end to the financial relationship between the parties in that case where it would be difficult and wasteful to obtain periodic maintenance. By contrast, the Supreme Court has held fast to the desirability of achieving finality in family law cases in as much as possible in *P. O'D. v. A. O'D.*[36]

- Litigants also adopted a "wait and see" approach and were reluctant to institute divorce proceedings which gave details concerning their current economic position to their spouse.

- Many litigants were and still are stuck in the backlog of legal aid cases.

- Some litigants "of modest means" who do not come within the legal aid remit still find divorce proceedings expensive.

- Some litigants who had stressful experiences on separation are very reluctant to open up "old wounds" unless they require the decree in order to remarry.

The were 417 divorce applications in 1997, while there were 2,765 applications in 1998. Again, it must be borne in mind that the Family Law (Divorce) Act came into operation at the end of February 1997 and the Department's statistical "year" ends July 31, 1997, one is not therefore comparing like with like. The statistical information indicates that 95 decrees of divorce were granted in 1997 ( 93 at Circuit Court level and 2 at High Court level) and 1,452 decrees were granted in 1998 ( 1,439 at Circuit Court level and 13 at High Court level. Preliminary figures issued by the Department for the periods August

---

[33] [1995] 2 I.R. 354.
[34] [1997] 3 I.R 64.
[35] Unreported, High Court, November 27, 1998 (1996, No. 103 Sp).
[36] [1998] 1 I.L.R.M. 543.

1, 1998 to 31 December, 1998 and January 1, 1999 to March 31, 1999 show that so far there have been 2,445 applications for divorce received at Circuit Court level and 1, 294 divorce decrees have been granted by the Circuit Court. The statistical year ends on July 31, 1999, however, and the High Court figures must be added to these figures and so all that can be said at this stage is that the figures for 1999 will probably show a moderate increase in the number of divorce applications received and granted. It is however, far too early to say whether this increase represents a "trend".

## PRACTICE ISSUES

As the vast majority of applications are at Circuit Court level I will confine my comments to Circuit Court practice and procedure. The Circuit Court Rules[37] cover all proceedings for divorce, judicial separation, relief after foreign divorce or separation outside the state, nullity, declarations of marital status, determination of property disputes between spouses pursuant to section 36 of the 1995 Act, disputes between formerly engaged couples under section 44 of the 1996 Act, and relief pursuant to section 25 and 15 A of the 1995 Act and section 18 of the 1996 Act. All such proceedings are instituted by a Family Law Civil Bill in the form set out in the Rules. Certain observations can be made in relation to the Civil Bill procedure:

- Significant information and detail must be obtained before the institution of the proceedings. A certified copy of the previous orders/agreements must be annexed to the Family Law Civil Bill. Details of the family home must contain title details, and pension details.

- The affidavit of means and welfare are quite detailed documents and also take time and trouble to prepare. They provide the Court with very important information enabling the Court to discharge its constitutional obligation to determine whether "adequate provision" has been made.

- The time limit allocated for the filing of the defence/counterclaim is very short bearing in mind the level of detail which must be provided.

---

[37] S.I. No. 84 of 1997.

- The default procedure is extremely useful to "prod on" ostrich type respondents. However where a defence is filed out of time on a motion, the respondent must pay the costs of the motion in the appropriate sum, whereas the practice which has developed on a first default before the County Registrar is that costs are rarely awarded.

- Discovery is frequently seen as a necessary step in cases where the main earner is not in PAYE employment or is self employed. Discovery can add substantially to the delay and costs in proceedings, see *E.P v. C.P.*[38] where McGuinness J. noted that discovery can sometimes be more trouble than it is worth. On the other hand practitioners face the dilemma of balancing the likely outcome of discovery against the costs of same. It is very difficult to judge in any case especially where the client firmly believes that there are substantial undisclosed assets.[39]

- The valuation of family companies can sometimes be very artificial especially where the company will not be sold, see *Potter v. Potter*,[40] *B. v. B.* (financial provision)[41] and *P. v. P.* (financial provision).[42] Private companies can be valued in a number of different ways,[43] see *Attorney General v. Jameson*,[44] *Re Clubman Shirts Ltd*,[45] *Colgan v. Colgan*[46] and *Irish Press plc v. Ingersol Irish Publications Ltd*.[47] Assessing the valuation of a spouse's shareholding is also a difficult task.[48]

In family law litigation costs rarely follow the event. The form of divorce which we have in Ireland is labour intensive in that the supporting documentation is complex. A court appearance is always re-

---

[38] Unreported, High Court, *ex tempore*, McGuinness J., Nov. 27, 1998.
[39] See Chapter 3.
[40] [1982] 2 All E.R. 321.
[41] [1989] 1 F.L.R. 241.
[42] [1989] 2 F.L.R. 241.
[43] See generally, Courtney, *The Law of Private Companies* (Butterworths, 1994).
[44] [1904] 2 I.R. 644.
[45] [1991] I.L.R.M. 43.
[46] Unreported. High Court, Costello J., July 22, 1993.
[47] Unreported, High Court, Barron J., May 13, 1994.
[48] See generally, Fox and Brown, *The Law of Private Companies* (Sweet & Maxwell, 1991), Chap. 14.

quired. It is not a matter of ticking boxes and receiving the decree through the post. The importance of costs has been highlighted in a number of leading U.K cases, in particular *Evans v. Evans*,[49] a decision of Booth J. In that case, the assets in issue were not substantial and yet both parties incurred substantial legal fees thereby diluting the available funds and making it impossible for the court to make appropriate provision for the parties. The court issued guidelines for practitioners in the conduct of ancillary relief cases. These guidelines were given with the concurrence of the President of the Family Law Division and are treated as a form of practice direction. They have also been incorporated in Guidelines of the Law Society and strictly enforced by the courts. In the U.K, the issue of "wasted costs" has also been litigated in a series of cases, so that costs are at the forefront of consideration in each and every case. The search to find all the assets can indeed sometimes be a fruitless exercise which only adds to the costs. On the other hand failure to bring out all the assets through the discovery process is equally appalling and needless to say dangerous. Practitioners must continue to balance the likely outcome of the discovery process against the costs incurred in pursuing same – never an easy task.

---

[49] [1990] 2 All E.R. 147.

# Chapter 2

# Maintenance, Property and Discovery

## *Stephanie Coggans\**

### MAINTENANCE

Maintenance is only one of a number of financial reliefs which may be sought by way of ancillary relief on application to the court for a decree of divorce. Because of the extent of this topic, it will be dealt with under the following headings:

1. legislative provisions – the Family Law (Divorce) Act 1996;

2. factors to be applied on the making of an order;

3. recent case law.

### Legislative Provisions

*Section 5(1) – Proper Provision*

Section 5(1) of the Family Law (Divorce) Act 1996 provides that before a decree of divorce may be granted, the Court must be satisfied that "such provision as the court considers proper having regard to the circumstances exists or will be made for the spouses and any dependent members of the family". The court is charged with the duty of ensuring that proper provision has been made in the particular circumstances of each case, and on foot of the wording of the constitutional amendment, this extends to "any children of either or both of (the spouses)".[1] Thus, it is open to the court, when agreed terms of settlement in relation to ancillary reliefs are placed before it for ruling in the context of an application for divorce, to refuse to

---

*\*Stephanie Coggans is the Solicitor in Charge, Law Centre, Cavan. She is co-author of The Family Law (Divorce) Act 1996 (annotated). She is a member of the Law Society of Ireland's Family Law and Civil Legal Aid Committee.*

[1]  See *C.(R.) v. C.(C.)* (1997) 1 F.L.R. 1 .

implement the settlement if not satisfied that proper provision has been made. Clients should therefore be advised that after settlement terms have been agreed by the parties, that these may be rejected by the court in exercising its jurisdiction under the Act. A problem which may arise in this regard is that a court may reject as insufficient provision which the parties have perhaps been implementing for some time by agreement, for example an agreed weekly maintenance payment. Such previous arrangements may be re-opened by the court, and reassessed although regard should be had to section 20(3) of the 1996 Act which states that the terms of a previous separation agreement still in force shall be taken into account by the court. Presumably, the terms of previous court orders which are also still in force would be taken into account by the court in deciding whether to make an order, particularly where both parties are satisfied with same.

## Section 12 – Maintenance Pending Suit

Section 12 of the Family Law (Divorce) Act 1996 provides for the making of interim orders for maintenance, which orders will cease to operate on the ultimate determination by the court of the application for a decree of divorce and ancillary reliefs. The order under section 12 may be backdated to the date the application was made, but not earlier, and the order may comprise periodical or lump sum payments. The court may, as in all maintenance orders, specify terms and conditions on the order, for example that a lump sum amount be used to discharge school fees.

## Section 13 – Periodical Payments and Lump Sum Orders

Section 13 of the Family Law (Divorce) Act 1996 allows for the making of periodical payments orders, secured periodical payments orders and lump sum orders. The orders may be made either at the time the decree is granted, or at any time thereafter. The application for relief may be made by either of the spouses, or by someone on behalf of a dependent member of the family. An order may be made for either a periodical payment, or lump sum, or both. A secured periodical payment order (and it appears that these are relatively rare) provides that the payments may be secured for example to a particular bank account, or to rental income from property.

Section 13(2) directs that a lump sum may be ordered to reimburse a spouse or dependent family member who has incurred expenses prior to the making of the application, for example for expenses incurred while maintenance was not being paid. Section 13(3) directs that a lump sum may be paid by way of instalments, secured or otherwise.

Periodical payments orders will cease on the death of the payee.[2] They will also cease on the remarriage of the payee. No maintenance orders under section 13 will be made in respect of a spouse who has remarried.[3] Section 13 also makes provision for attachment of earnings orders, and for variation of those orders under section 22 of the 1996 Act if necessary.

## Section 21– Retrospective Periodical Payments Orders

Section 21 of the Family Law (Divorce) Act 1996 permits the backdating of an order for periodical payments, to a date not earlier than the making of the application for a decree of divorce. It is to be distinguished from the retrospection available under section 12(1), which refers specifically to maintenance pending suit.

## Section 22 – Variation Provisions

Any order made in respect of maintenance may be varied pursuant to the provisions of this section, with the exception of a lump sum payment which is not being paid in instalments. The class of person who may make an application under this section has been extended from the payees of any orders to include, in the case of the remarriage of either of the spouses, the new spouse. Before varying any order under section 22, the court must have regard to any change of circumstances which may have occurred, or any new evidence which there may be. In addition to varying or discharging any order previously made, the court may suspend the operation of the order for a period of time. In the Circuit Court case of *S. (R.) v. S. (R.)*[4] McGuinness J. commented that orders in respect of maintenance are always open to variation, even aside from the variation provisions contained in the Act in question, which was the 1989 Act. Similar sentiments were expressed by Barr J. in the case of *G.H. v. E.H.*[5] in refusing an appli-

---

[2] s. 13(4).
[3] s. 13(5).
[4] (1996) 3 Fam. L.J. 92.
[5] Unreported, High Court, Barr J., Feb. 9, 1998.

cation for a downward variation in maintenance as the respondent's circumstances had not changed since the original order.

### Section 23 – Conduct

Section 23 of the Family Law (Divorce) Act 1996 states that where a maintenance order is being made or varied on behalf of a dependent family member, the issue of conduct on behalf of either of the spouses will not be relevant.

### Section 24 – Terms and Conditions

Section 24 of the Family Law (Divorce) Act 1996 permits a court to attach terms and conditions to, *inter alia*, orders for maintenance made under the 1996 Act.

### Section 25 – Stay Pending Appeal

Section 25 of the Family Law (Divorce) Act 1996 directs that an order made under section 12 or section 13(1) or section 22(l) (a), (b) or (c) which is subsequently appealed, will not be subject to an automatic stay unless the court which made the order or the court to which the appeal is made directs otherwise. This provision also applies to District Court orders for maintenance and accordingly a stay on the operation of a maintenance order should be sought if an appeal is contemplated.

### Section 26 – Orders Made Under Other Legislation

Section 26 of the Family Law (Divorce) Act 1996 provides that orders for maintenance made pursuant to other legislation may be either continued or discharged by an order under this section.

### Section 28 – Transmission of Periodical Payments

Section 28 of the Family Law (Divorce) Act 1996 permits the transmission of periodical payments made under the 1996 Act to be made through the District Court Clerk. This is a most useful provision to ensure regular payments, and to provide a record of all payments made.

*Section 30 – Enforcement of Court Orders Act 1940*

Section 30 of the Family Law (Divorce) Act 1996 extends the provisions of the Enforcement of Court Orders Act 1940 to maintenance orders made under the 1996 Act.

## Factors to be taken into account

*Section 20*

The criteria set out in section 20 of the Family Law (Divorce) Act 1996 are to be applied by the court in the making of orders for financial relief (and other ancillary orders). The provisions of section 20 act as a guide to the court in ensuring that proper provision is made for the appropriate parties, and also as a guide to practitioners in advising their clients what orders may ultimately be made by the court. The application of the corresponding provisions of section 16 of the 1995 Act were considered by McGuinness J. in *J.(D.) v. D.(D.).*[6] The provisions of this section are largely similar to the provisions of section 20 of the 1996 Act, although with some important differences, commencing with the standard of provision to be levied by the court in terms of financial relief, which on divorce is "proper provision" and on judicial separation is "adequate and reasonable provision". McGuinness J. reviewed section 16 in detail in the course of her judgment and commented that "even given these guidelines . . . the court still has a wide area of discretion, particularly in cases where there are considerable financial assets".

McGuinness J. also dealt with the issue of conduct[7] which in that case comprised admitted adultery by the husband and an effort by him to secrete assets. The court felt in this instance that no injustice would be done by disregarding the adultery, and given that an order pursuant to section 35 of the 1996 Act was being made, this disposed of the issue of financial misconduct.

It should be noted that while conduct is only one of a number of issues set out in section 20 to be taken into account on the making of financial relief orders, the court must address conduct but will not usually make punitive orders on foot of it. The factor set out at section 20(2)(l) which alludes to "the rights of any person other than the

---

[6] [1997] 3 I.R. 64.
[7] s. 20(2)(i) of the Family Law (Divorce) Act 1996.

spouses but including a person to whom either spouse is remarried",
is not new but appeared in the Family Law Act 1995 in relation to
persons who had obtained foreign divorces and subsequently re-married.

### Recent Case Law

The case of *E.P. v. C.P.*[8] concerned applications for both judicial
separation and divorce, both of which were granted. There was a
high degree of conflict between the parties, and a fairly complicated
financial background. This case demonstrated the obligation on judges
to have the peace keeping and negotiating skills of the United Nations. In relation to maintenance, the court stated that ". . . the most
important factor in this case is the security and maintenance of the
children". McGuinness J. agreed with the wife that a "large lump
sum would be a desirable solution, and that it may indeed be difficult
and wasteful to obtain periodic maintenance". This was because it
appeared unlikely, from the history of non-compliance with previous
maintenance orders, that the husband would make regular periodic
payments. A lump sum order was made in the circumstances.

The case of *JCN v. RTN*[9] concerned an elderly couple who, having entered into a separation agreement in 1975, were now seeking a
divorce, the wife having instituted the proceedings seeking, *inter alia*,
financial relief by way of maintenance and a lump sum. In 1996, an
order for maintenance was made on consent in the High Court, and
the court considered that the best option was to continue the terms of
that maintenance order. The court also decided not to make a lump
sum order, as the capital sum in the husband's possession was not
large enough, and the family home had been sold on separation and
the proceeds divided. It was stated that:

> "at present interest rates, only a large capital sum would provide the
> wife with an appreciable investment income, and this would leave the
> husband without the capital which he needs to finance his own household and the educational expense of his dependent children (from his
> second relationship) for whom provision must also be made."

In order to leave the wife with security in relation to future maintenance payments should her husband pre-decease her, the court ad-

---

[8]   High Court, *ex tempore*, McGuinness J., November 27, 1998.
[9]   Unreported, High Court, McGuinness J., January 15, 1999.

justed the husband's pension entitlements to pay half of the annual sum to the wife, and the other half to the husband's partner.

The case of *G.H v. E.H.*[10] involved an application for a downward variation in maintenance which was refused as the respondent's circumstances had not changed since the original order. The applicant was entitled to a reasonable lifestyle commensurate with that of the respondent. The respondent had attempted to evade his liability to pay maintenance, and had unilaterally reduced the maintenance on more than one occasion.

The case of *J.D. v. D.D.*[11] concerned an application for judicial separation, but in the course of her judgment, McGuinness J. explored in detail the issue of financial provision on marriage breakdown, and entered into a detailed analysis of the issue of whether or not a clean break could be provided post judicial separation and divorce. The case involved a 30-year marriage where there were considerable financial resources. The decree was granted on the basis of the husband's adultery and a lack of a normal marital relationship for a year. The learned judge declared the principal issue between the parties to be the level and form of maintenance to be paid to the wife. She applied the provisions of section 16 of the 1995 Act to the circumstances of the case, and went on to consider "whether it is open to this court to endeavour to create a situation of finality . . . by making a sizeable lump sum order in favour of the wife and making no order for periodic maintenance". McGuinness opined as follows:

> ". . . it appears to me that by the subsequent enactment of the Family Law Act, 1995 and the Family Law (Divorce) Act, 1996, the Oireachtas has made it clear that a 'clean break' situation is not to be sought and that, if anything, financial finality is virtually to be prevented. . . . The statutory policy is, therefore, totally opposed to the concept of the 'clean break'."

The court ordered a lump sum payment by way of maintenance, in addition to the husband financing the wife's residence, and a periodical payment of £20,000 per annum.

The issue of whether our jurisprudence has adapted to the changes in the law since the enactment of divorce has led to much debate, particularly in relation to the issue of whether there can ever be finality concerning post-divorce financial arrangements. In the *Irish Jour-*

---

[10] Unreported, High Court, Barr J., February 9 1998.
[11] Unreported, High Court, McGuinness J., May 14, 1997.

*nal of Family Law*[12] Conor Power cogently argues that the introduction of divorce should have brought about a reassessment of the
basis on which maintenance is paid to former spouses, but this did
not happen. Particularly in relation to divorce, whether or not a clean
break may be facilitated by orders for financial provision will be of
concern to practitioners, regardless of whether they act for those seeking or those attempting to avoid a clean break. In this regard, we are
referring specifically to spousal support as the financial obligations
to dependent family members are a different matter.

The fact that on divorce, the parties are legally "free" of each
other is not borne out where continuing financial provision remains
in place, particularly given that parties will be living separate and
apart for a minimum of four years. The position of a spouse who, for
example, has had no contact with the other spouse for ten years, and
who has built up a successful business since the marriage ended, will
be threatened if that other spouse institutes proceedings seeking a
decree of divorce and ancillary reliefs, specifically, periodic and lump
sum maintenance. The fact that the legislation is underpinned with a
rationale of financial need, coupled with judicial determination as to
the lack of a clean break means that in all likelihood, orders for relief
will be made. The question is, should a former spouse be obliged to
maintain a former spouse?

On the other hand, take the situation where an applicant spouse
has, for the last five years, survived with the assistance of maintenance payments from a financially secure spouse and now faces an
application for a downward variation in maintenance payments which
will leave him or her less financially secure. In those circumstances,
should maintenance payments be continued? Is the requirement of
proper provision the overriding criteria, to the exclusion of a consideration of the position of the paying spouse, who may have acquired
further dependents and financial obligations?

Power argues in his article cited above that other bases for award-
ing maintenance should be explored, and that ". . . a proper aim for
the continuing obligations must be found; to have equal misery is not
to seek equal misery".[13] The reality is that financial certainty on divorce is not there for the asking, not facilitated on the face of things
by the legislation and by judicial pronouncement, and not something
for which there would necessarily be widespread approval.

---

[12] Power, "Maintenance: No Clean Break with the Past" (1998) 1 I.F.L.J. 15.
[13] *ibid.*

## PROPERTY

Property adjustment orders have been part of Irish law since the coming into operation of section 15 of the Judicial Separation and Family Law Reform Act 1989. When Part II of the 1989 Act was repealed, property adjustment orders were enshrined in section 9 of the Family Law Act 1995, which was subsequently amended by section 52(b) of the Family Law (Divorce) Act 1996, which permitted the seeking of a property adjustment order (PAO) either at the time the decree of judicial separation was granted, or at any time thereafter. This power was not available to those who had obtained a PAO pursuant to the provisions of the 1989 Act.

### When will a PAO be granted?

On divorce, a PAO will be granted pursuant to section 14 of the Family Law (Divorce) Act 1996. The PAO may be granted either at the time the decree is granted, or at any time thereafter during the lifetime of the other spouse.

### Who can apply for a PAO on divorce?

1. Either spouse.

2. A person on behalf of a dependent family member.

### What kinds of orders may be obtained?

1. A transfer of property from one spouse to another, or from one spouse to a dependent family member or to a person to hold property for the benefit of that dependent family member.

2. A settlement of specified property for the benefit of one spouse or a dependent family member.

3. A variation of a post or ante-nuptial settlement, for the benefit of either of the spouses or dependent family members.

4. An extinguishment or reduction of the interest of either of the spouses under any such settlement.

### What is property?

Property includes both real and personal property; for example, houses, shares, investments, bank deposits, car, antiques, art, jewellery and animals. The property may be owned outright, or may be held by way of an interest in possession or reversion; the property may be held by way of legal or beneficial ownership, or co-ownership, either with the other spouse or with a third party. Accordingly, a tenancy in a premises may be transferred and where necessary care should be taken to ensure that an exclusion order is obtained pursuant to section 15(1)(a) of the 1996 Act in those circumstances.

### Are there restrictions on the making of PAOs set out in section 14?

Section 14(2) sets out restrictions on the application of section 22 of the Family Law (Divorce) Act 1996 (the section dealing with variation of orders made under Part III) to orders made under section 14(1)(b), (c), or (d). Section 14(3) decrees that no PAO will be made in respect of a spouse who has remarried since the decree of divorce was granted. Section 14 (7) provides that no PAO will be made in respect of a family home in which either of the spouses, having remarried since the decree was granted, now lives with their new spouse.

### How often can applications for PAOs be made?

The terms of the legislation appear to envisage the making of any number of PAOs, in relation to any number of properties if relevant to the terms of the case. In practice, probably the most common form of PAO is a simple transfer of property from one spouse to another. Such an order cannot subsequently be varied by an application under section 22 of the Act, although it may of course be varied on appeal. An order made under section 14(1), (b), (c), or (d) may be varied by an application under section 22 *provided* the applicability of section 22 to that order has not been restricted by an order under section 14(2).

### What factors are applied by the court in deciding whether to make a PAO?

The basic approach of the court will be to attempt, by the making of a PAO and other ancillary orders, to ensure that proper provision has been made for the relevant parties. The court will also take into account the factors set out in section 20 of the Act, which include the terms of any separation agreement which are still in force,[14] and the rights of any new spouses. The court will not, pursuant to the provisions of section 20(5) of the Act, make a PAO unless it would be "in the interests of justice to do so".

## Do post-nuptial settlements referred to in section 14 (1) of the Act include separation agreements?

The answer is "yes". On divorce, the court may vary either the terms of a separation agreement, or the terms of ancillary orders made in the context of a decree of judicial separation. The court is directed to take into account the terms of a separation agreement entered into by the spouses and which is still in force. This situation should be distinguished from that which pertains on judicial separation, where pursuant to the case of *P. O'D. v. A. O'D.*,[15] it was held that the existence of a binding and valid separation agreement precluded the issue of an application to court for a judicial separation.

In the case of *B.S. v. J.S.*,[16] the applicant wife sought a decree of divorce, together with ancillary reliefs including a PAO to transfer the family home of the parties into her sole name. On January 18, 1993, a decree of judicial separation had been granted to the parties together with various ancillary orders, on consent between the parties, one of which directed that the family home be held by the parties as tenants in common, with the wife to have a right of residence therein for her life to the exclusion of the husband. White J. declared himself satisfied to have the power to vacate former orders, particularly when granting a decree of divorce, and went on to direct a transfer of the family home into the sole name of the applicant wife, subject to the mortgage in favour of Mayo County Council. It is my understanding that this decision is the subject of an appeal by the husband.

On any application for a decree of divorce with ancillary reliefs, any orders made will be new orders, as opposed to a discharge or vacation of orders previously made. However, the provisions of sec-

---

[14] s. 20(3).
[15] [1998] 1 I.L.R.M. 543.
[16] Unreported, Circuit Court, White J., February 5, 1999.

tion 26 of the 1996 Act may apply in circumstances where ancillary reliefs have been made pursuant to the Acts of 1989 and 1995, and which ancillary orders are still in place. In those circumstances, the court may by order discharge the orders made under those Acts, from such date as may be specified in the order (section 21(l)).

It is also open to the Court to leave orders previously made pursuant to the Acts of 1976, 1989 and 1995 in force. Indeed, section 26(2) of the Family Law (Divorce) Act 1996 provides that where an order under any of these Acts is in force, and a decree of divorce is granted, the order previously made continues in force unless it is discharged by an order pursuant to section 26(1). Any such orders remaining so in force may be varied by section 22 of the 1996 Act.

Thus it can be seen that in circumstances where orders continue in force to the satisfaction of all parties and to the satisfaction of the court, those orders may be left in being and a simple decree of divorce granted thus obviating the need for difficulty. In order to avoid all doubt, particularly in circumstances where the terms of ancillary reliefs on divorce are agreed between the parties, the court should be asked to discharge or confirm the orders previously made which are now to continue to operate in the context of the post divorce situation. Section 26 is silent as to the effect of orders previously made in a higher court.

### What other orders may be made specifically in relation to property?

Pursuant to section 11 of the 1996 Act, an order may be made under sections 5 or 9 of the Family Home Protection Act 1976. Section 5 of the 1976 Act allows the court to make orders for the protection of the Family Home in the interest of an applicant spouse or child where the other spouse is engaging in such conduct as may lead to the loss of any interest in the family home, or render it unsuitable for habitation as a family home. Section 9 of the 1976 Act permits the court to make orders prohibiting the removal by one of the spouses of household chattels from the family home. Section 11 of the 1996 Act is similar in its terms to section 11 of the 1989 Act.

In the case of *A.S. v. G.S. and Allied Irish Banks plc.*(notice party),[17] the applicant wife obtained an interlocutory order pursuant to section 11(c) of the 1989 Act preventing the registration of a judg-

---

[17] Unreported, High Court, Geoghegan J., February 2, 1994.

ment mortgage pending the hearing of judicial separation proceedings. The Bank subsequently sought the lifting of the section 11 order to enable it to register its judgment mortgage. The court refused to lift the section 11 order prior to the making of a property adjustment order. The court held that the applicant's claim to a property adjustment order was a *lis pendens* registerable under the 1844 Act even though the claim was contingent upon the court deciding to make such an order. A property adjustment order made by the court would have priority over any judgment mortgage which the Bank might have registered beforehand.

. Section 15(1)(a) permits the court to make an order against either spouse, excluding them from the family home for life, or for another specified period. Section 15(1)(a)(ii) permits the court to make an order directing that the family home be sold and the proceeds of sale divided between the spouses. The court may also make orders pursuant to section 36 of the 1995 Act, which enables the court to determine disputes as to title to or possession of property based on the principle of who paid for the property by direct or indirect financial contributions (section 15(1)(b)).

The court can also make orders under sections 5, 7 or 9 of the Family Home Protection Act 1976 (section 15(1)(c)) and under the Partition Acts (section 15(1)(e)). The court is directed by the provisions of section 15(2) to take account of the fact that where a decree of divorce is granted, it is not possible for the spouses concerned to reside together, and that proper and secure accommodation should be provided for the parties concerned.

It is not possible to have an exclusion order made in respect of a family home in which, following the grant of a decree of divorce, one of the spouses concerned is living with their new spouse.

### What are the conveyancing implications of a property adjustment order?

Once a property adjustment order has been made in relation to land, a copy of that order must be lodged by the Registrar or Clerk of the Court in the Land Registry for registration pursuant to the Registration of Title Act 1964. In the event that the land is registered in the registry of deeds, a copy of the order concerned will be forwarded to the registry of deeds. Accordingly, clear details as to title and description of land should be set out in the pleadings to facilitate the drawing up of the relevant orders.

Section 14(5) deals with a situation which may occur when the person directed by court order to transfer the lands in question refuses to do so. In those circumstances, the court may order another person to execute the relevant deeds to give effect to the order. Most frequently, orders in this regard are made directing the county registrar to do so. It is becoming common for such an order to be sought at the time the property transfer order is made. The court may also specify that a period of time will be allowed for the spouse to sign the relevant documentation, and at the expiry of that period, the county registrar may then sign.

The issue of who pays the costs of placing a property for sale, and the conveyancing costs can frequently cause problems. As we have already seen, the court may make an order pursuant to section 14(6) in relation to such costs, and where difficulties can be foreseen in this regard it is wise to have such an order made.

In the case of *O'L.(A.). v. O'L. (B.),*[18] a property adjustment order was made in respect of the family home, and it was directed that the respective solicitors of the parties were to have joint carriage of sale. McGuinness J. referred to the decision of *J.D. v. P.D.,*[19] and stated that the joint carriage of the sale should be on condition that the joint charges of the solicitors in respect of the sale should not exceed the charges which would be proper if one only had carriage.

## DISCOVERY

An application for discovery is a pre-trial device which enables either of the parties to a dispute to gain disclosure of information, usually, but not limited to, financial information. To properly prepare a case for hearing, and to accurately advise clients about the possible orders which could be made by the court, it is necessary to have as complete a picture as possible of the financial position of both parties. This section will concentrate on financial disclosure which is the most frequent target of discovery applications, but one must keep in mind the fact that discovery of other kinds of information may also be sought.

Discovery also aids the court, which requires information to be placed before it in cogent, digestible form. In the case of *L.(J.) v.*

---

[18] Circuit Court, McGuinness J., November 23, 1995.
[19] Unreported, High Court, August 9, 1994.

*L.(J.)*[20] McGuinness J. was displayed her dissatisfaction at being obliged to trawl through large amounts of discovery documentation to attempt to find information which should have been set out in the affidavit of means, a task which she stated was not the business of the trial judge. She stated:

> "Although the financial issues are of prime importance in this case the financial evidence before the court was of a most confusing and unsatisfactory nature. . . . During the trial a great deal of time was spent in detailed cross-examination of both parties arising out of the discovery of documents. Finally the entire documents were handed into court. . . . However what was entirely lacking was a clear and systematic picture of the present financial position of each parties assets and liabilities, resources and needs."

This is a clear judicial pronouncement as to what should emerge from properly constructed discovery.

## The Affidavit of Means

Discovery is not usually sought until after delivery of the defence and affidavits of means and welfare by both sides as it will not be known until that time what information is being delivered.[21] Where financial relief is being sought in applications for judicial separation and divorce both spouses are required to file an affidavit of means setting out specified information. The specimen affidavit in appendix 1 is completed showing all information required. Such an affidavit is required only where financial relief is being sought and this includes situations where the only form of relief being sought is an order pursuant to section 18 of the Family Law (Divorce) Act 1996, where what is required is an order blocking the other spouse from seeking provision out of the estate of the spouse on that spouse's death. The necessity of filing the affidavit in such circumstances, and indeed in circumstances where parties have been separated for a long time, has not been welcomed by some parties who would see the provision of such information as at best unnecessary and at worst likely to lead to temptation. Information set out in the affidavit of means may be vouched and should be so vouched within 14 days of

---

[20] (1996) 1 Fam L.J. 36.
[21] The Rules of the Superior Courts (No. 3) of 1997 (S.I. No. 84 of 1997) for High Court applications, and the Rules of the Circuit Court 1991, (S.I. No. 159 of 1991) for Circuit Court applications.

the request to do so. If such a request is not complied with, the court may make an order directing compliance or directing discovery.

However, it is undoubtedly the case that properly completed affidavits of means should yield sufficient financial information in cases where the financial position of the parties is not complicated. In the case of *L.(J.) v. L.(J.)*, referred to above, the court stated that if the "financial framework of the affidavits is missing, the process of examination and cross examination based on the discovery materials can be both confusing and unproductive as indeed was the position in this case". In addition, we are all familiar with the client convinced that thorough discovery will yield lotto winnings, the house in France and the third party's address, and this constitutes an abuse of the discovery process and should be discouraged by practitioners.

### Voluntary Discovery

Where additional information is required, it should firstly be sought on a voluntary basis. Order 31, rule 12(4) of the Superior Court Rules provides that either party may request the other, in writing, to make voluntary discovery of all relevant documents, which if so agreed must be made within a reasonable period of time. The requesting party may also agree to provide discovery, and affidavits of discovery in the proper format prescribed by the rules may be sworn and exchanged.[22]

If an agreement for voluntary discovery is made between parties, it has the same effect as though ordered by the court. Failure to comply with the agreement will be brought to the attention of the court in any subsequent application for discovery that may be made.

### Application to Court

If voluntary discovery is not forthcoming, or in circumstances where it is necessary to apply to court for an order for discovery, such an application will be made pursuant to section 38(6) and (7) of the Family Law (Divorce) Act 1996.[23]

---

[22] R.S.C. 1986, Ord.31, r.13.
[23] Section 38(6) states:
   "In proceedings under *section 13, 14, 15 (1) (a), 16, 17, 18* or *22* –
   (a) each of the spouses concerned shall give to the other spouse and to, or

The important words in section 38(6) are "as may reasonably be required". This is an attempt by the legislature to ensure that parties, and practitioners, do not become over zealous in their quest for information, incurring large costs in the process. Clients need to be advised of the potential for spiraling costs involved in repeated applications to court, and this has been the subject of judicial comment, most clearly in the case of *E.P. v. C.P.* referred to above.[24] This case involved an application both for judicial separation and divorce. There were repeated applications for orders for attachment and committal by the wife of the husband, and repeated adjournments on the grounds that discovery was not complete. The court stated that: "in this type of family law case (and I and other judges have said it before) discovery can sometimes be, to put it in plain language, more trouble than it is worth." Going on to comment that the wife's actions in relation to discovery were understandable in the circumstances of the case, which were very acrimonious, McGuinness J. nonetheless stated that ". . . long delays for extra discovery may well be counterproductive in these cases".

The application for discovery will be made by way of notice of motion, not necessarily grounded on affidavit, to either the County Registrar at first instance, or to the Circuit Court or to the Master of the High Court. The Court has discretion in the event of a dispute to decide whether an order should be made and in what terms, for example, for how many years the discovery is to refer. The court may also rule on the relevance of certain documents or categories of documents, as arose in the case of *L.(T.) v. L. (V.)*.[25] In that case, (an application for judicial separation) general orders for discovery were granted in June 1994 to cover a period of three years. An issue arose as to the non-production of a diary or notebook which was alleged to

---

to a person acting on behalf of, any dependent member of the family concerned, and
(b) any dependent member of the family concerned shall give to, or to a person acting on behalf of, any other such member and to each of the spouses concerned,
such particulars of his or her property and income as may reasonably be required for the purposes of the proceedings."
Section 38(7) states:
"Where a person fails or refuses to comply with *subsection* (6), the court on application to it in that behalf by a person having an interest in the matter, may direct the person to comply with that subsection."

[24] Unreported, High Court, *ex tempore*, McGuinness J., November 27, 1998.
[25] (1995) 1 Fam. L.J. 7.

have contained information about the respondents private medical practice. Pocket diaries were produced but privilege was claimed in respect of parts of them as they contained notes made by the respondent at the suggestion of his solicitor concerning the parties and their children, which notes were made specifically for the preparation of the trial. The applicant on the other hand argued that the welfare of the children took precedence over legal professional privilege. It was held by McGuinness J. that "in each case the desirability of discovery on the facts must be weighed against the desirability of maintaining legal professional privilege and a decision taken in the light of the interests of the child. The privilege should only rarely be overridden and only when the court is satisfied it is necessary." McGuinness J. also commented (*obiter*) that in suitable circumstances and in particular in the case of medical/expert reports where the welfare of a child is in issue, the court has the power to override legal professional privilege.

## The Affidavit of Discovery

There seems to be an understanding on the part of some practitioners that in family law cases, "real" affidavits of discovery do not have to be sworn, and that the only necessary form of discovery is to produce a completed affidavit of means. This is not the case, and in all cases affidavits to be filed should be sworn in compliance with the rules, in the High Court in accordance with Form 10 set out in Appendix C of the Rules of the Superior Court, and in the Circuit Court as set out in the schedule to the rules. For obvious reasons, discovery is not a feature of District Court cases, but it could only be of greater assistance to all participants if statements of means were to be produced as a matter of course in the context of all applications for financial relief.

Once exchanged, and filed, the discovery documents of each party may be inspected by the client and by their legal advisors, and copies of necessary documents obtained. The affidavit must set out all documents in the power, possession or procurement of each party, with explanations as to why certain documents are not being provided, if that is the case. Discovery should not be provided in a haphazard fashion, and efforts should be made to ensure ease of reference to the information, for example by listing categories of documentation together. Nor should vast quantities of documentation be delivered in an attempt to "snow" the other side.

In deciding what to discover, practitioners should refer again to the wording of section 38(6), which directs the production of "such particulars of ... property and income as may reasonably be required for the purposes of the proceedings". By adhering to these directions this should have the effect of limiting the documentation to be set out in the affidavit of discovery, and also of limiting the expectations of the client in relation to discovery, which sometimes can be less than realistic.

If a spouse is unhappy with what is yielded by discovery, they may seek further and better discovery, by way of application to court if necessary after a request for such information has not succeeded. There must be proper reasons for seeking additional discovery and not simply a belief by one of the spouses that information is being withheld.

Sometimes, discovery against a third party will be necessary, where that party has in their possession, power or procurement documentation relevant to the issues in the case between the parties. The important word here is "relevant", and the court must be convinced of the relevance of the documentation being sought before it will make an order for third party discovery, pursuant to Order 29 of the Rules of the Superior Courts. One of the features of an application for third party discovery is that the affidavit grounding same must include an undertaking in relation to the reasonable costs incurred by the party making the discovery, and clients must be made aware of additional costs involved.

## Privilege

As we have already seen, legal professional privilege may be claimed by a party swearing an affidavit in relation to producing certain documentation, specifically any communication to or from a legal advisor, and we refer in this regard to the decision of McGuinness J. in *L.(T.) v. L.(V.)* [26] set out above. In that case, McGuinness J. commented that "most solicitors and counsel who regularly practice in the field of family law will be familiar with the advice which is frequently given to matrimonial litigants to keep careful notes of current developments and happenings, both as they affect the parties, and more importantly, as they affect the children. These notes are made for the specific purpose of instructing a solicitor and counsel

---

[26] (1995) 1 Fam. L.J. 7.

and as preparation for the trial of the action." It was held that the notes which came into that category in that case fell to be covered by legal professional privilege.

McGuinness J., in the course of her judgment, comprehensively reviewed the English authorities in the area of privilege attaching to documentation concerning the welfare of children. She concluded, "that in suitable circumstances where the welfare of a child is in issue, the court has the power to override legal professional privilege. This would be particularly so in the case of medical or other expert's reports". She refused discovery of the disputed notes in the case, while noting that the Court will override usual privilege when satisfied that it is necessary to do so.

### After Discovery has been made

After discovery has been made or exchanged, it will be necessary to analyse the information provided with a view to advising the client about potential orders which may be made. It may be necessary to enlist the services of a forensic accountant, an auctioneer or valuer, an actuary, a tax consultant, a pension consultant, or insurance advisor. The costs involved in so doing may be considerable, and a decision to involve expert witnesses must be taken with a view to balancing the usefulness of their advices with the costs incurred in obtaining same. No guidelines have yet been issued by either the legislature or the judiciary in Ireland in relation to attempting to find this balance between the costs of frequently protracted discovery procedures and the value of the issues on the case, in comparison to the United Kingdom where in the case of *Evans v. Evans*[27] a series of guidelines were set out to assist practitioners.

Indeed, prior to seeking discovery, practitioners and their clients should conduct their own investigations, for example by making appropriate searches in the Land Registry or Registry of Deeds, by carrying out judgment searches against the parties, and by obtaining as much documentation as possible from one's own client. Valuations of property may be requisitioned, where possible by agreement with the other side.

---

[27] (1990) 1 F.L.R. 319.

## Inadmissible Evidence

Section 9 of the Family Law (Divorce) Act 1996 provides that evidential privilege is conferred on communications made in the course of reconciliation counselling, mediation, and ". . . efforts . . . to reach agreement between (the parties) on some or all of the terms of a separation or a divorce (whether or not made in the presence or with the knowledge of the other spouse). . . ." Section 45 of the 1996 Act introduces a similar provision to the 1995 Act. Obviously, this is a desirable provision, leaving parties free to engage in reconciliation and settlement talks without fear of disclosure of the contents of those communications by any third parties.

## Bankers Books Evidence

The provisions of the Bankers Books Evidence Acts 1879 and 1959 allow the court to grant an order that the applicant spouse or their legal representative may travel to named banks or building societies to look at accounts held by the other spouse. The application is made on an *ex parte* basis and is a useful, although cumbersome, device where no progress is being made in obtaining information. It is useful where there is a suspicion that accounts are being held under different names. Care should be taken when making the application to court to ask for an order allowing copies of the accounts to be taken away, as the financial institutions may refuse such request in the absence of a specific order to that effect. Costs will obviously be a big factor here.

## Duties of Practitioners

We are all familiar with the client who seeks advice in relation to how to minimise their exposure to financial disclosure. Clear advice must therefore be given in relation to the provisions of section 38(6) and (7) which provide that where a form of financial relief is being sought by way of ancillary orders, that "particulars of his or her property for the purposes of the proceedings" shall be furnished by the appropriate parties. In default of compliance with section 38(6), the court may direct compliance by an order made under section 38(7). In addition, the provisions of section 37 of the 1996 Act should be outlined to a reluctant client, explaining to them the power of the court in relation to transactions intended to prevent or reduce relief available to the other spouse. This section aims to prevent a spouse from reducing their assets with a view to depriving the other spouse of ancillary reliefs which could be granted. An injunction may be granted by the court against a spouse if they attempt to do this, and assets may be frozen by order of the court until the hearing of the action. There will obviously be further repercussions for the defaulting spouse if such an order is made as he or she will have shown his or her true colours to the court.

## DISCOVERY/CHECKLIST

| |
|---|
| ✓ Carry out all preliminary investigations possible. |
| ✓ Seek voluntary discovery/agree to cross discovery if necessary. |
| ✓ Review all material provided by voluntary discovery before seeking court orders. Attempt to agree matters, for example, valuations of property. |
| ✓ Advise the client as to the issue of costs, and that discovery is not a "fishing expedition". |
| ✓ Make an application to court pursuant to section 38(6) and (7). |
| ✓ On receipt of documentation, assess whether settlement may be attempted, or ensure documentation is properly presented to the court. Attempt agreement with the other side as to what documentation should be presented to the court. |

# Chapter 3

# Divorce – A View from the North

## *Claire Archbold**

## INTRODUCTION

While this book's subject matter is divorce in the Republic of Ireland, this chapter is intended to put the debate into a slightly different context, by providing a view from the North – the part of Ireland which has longer term experience of divorce law in practice. It aims to paint a picture of what happens in the divorce courts in the North, the issues which have emerged as important in that jurisdiction, and the directions which are being taken on some of the most current issues. Family law is an area in which a wider perspective is useful – family problems are universal. As in Dublin, law reformers in Belfast are increasingly looking to other jurisdictions; Australia, America, Canada, as well as to London, Edinburgh and Dublin for ideas as to the best way to fashion a family law system which will meet the needs of the people using it as fully as possible. Certain aspects of the two family law systems on the island of Ireland are very different – the "clean break" basis of ancillary relief in the North, as compared to the "sufficient provision" basis in the South is one example. However, other aspects of our family law systems may reveal similarities.

## THE LAW OF DIVORCE

### Divorce in Northern Ireland

The most useful starting point is clearly to outline the law on divorce in Northern Ireland, and the debate about the development of divorce law. Divorce in Northern Ireland is governed by the Matrimonial

*Claire Archbold is a barrister and lecturer in family law in Queens University, Belfast. She is also a qualified mediator and a researcher for the Office of Law Reform. She is a co-author of Unravelling the System: Divorce in Northern Ireland (The Stationery Office, Belfast, forthcoming).

Causes (NI) Order 1978. It is a "mixed" system, containing elements of both fault and no-fault divorce. Although the single ground for divorce is irretrievable breakdown of the marriage, evidence of this may only be provided in five ways, by showing:

1.  that the respondent had committed adultery;

2.  that the respondent had behaved in such a way that the petitioner cannot reasonably be expected to live with them;

3.  that the respondent had deserted the petitioner for a continuous period of at least two years;

4.  that the parties have been living separately for two years and the respondent consents to the divorce;

5.  that the parties have been living separately for five years.[1]

Like the English Act of 1973[2] on which it was based, the Matrimonial Causes Order was a compromise. Divorce has in effect been available in what is now Northern Ireland since long before partition. Parliamentary divorce – the passage of a private Act of Parliament dissolving the marriage – was available to those who could afford it, first from the United Kingdom Parliament at Westminster, then, after 1922, from the Northern Ireland Parliament at Stormont. Judicial remedies for matrimonial discord; nullity and judicial separation; were available from the Ecclesiastical Courts, and after 1877 from the High Court.[3] The position before judicial divorce was introduced was well-summed up by an English commentator of 1839, who said:

> "A man with a very large sum of money may get a divorce from the Houses of Parliament and may marry again. A man with a smaller but considerable sum of money may get from the Ecclesiastical Courts a half divorce which relieves him merely from his wife's debts but does not enable him to enter into another matrimonial connection. A man with no money, or an insufficient income, can have no divorce at all."[4]

Divorce on the sole ground of adultery (or aggravated adultery if the petitioner was a wife) had been available in England from 1857,[5] and

---

[1]   Matrimonial Causes (NI) Order 1978, Art. 3(2).
[2]   Matrimonial Causes Act 1973.
[3]   Supreme Court of Judicature (Ireland) Act 1877.
[4]   (1839) *Crim. Con. Gazette* 2:75.
[5]   Matrimonial Causes Act 1857.

although judicial review had not been extended to Ireland, the House of Lords (and subsequently the Stormont Parliament) granted Parliamentary divorces on the same ground. When widened grounds for divorce were introduced in England in 1937,[6] the Northern Ireland Parliament took the opportunity to replace the "grotesque and expensive"[7] Parliamentary procedure with a more rational judicial one. There was little social debate around the 1939 Act, although wider constitutional issues made occasional appearances in Parliamentary debate. The grounds for judicial divorce in the Matrimonial Causes Act (NI) 1939 were that:

1. the respondent had committed adultery;

2. the respondent had deserted the petitioner for three years;

3. the respondent had treated the petitioner with cruelty;

4. the respondent was incurably of unsound mind and had been receiving treatment for at least five years.[8]

The issue which attracted most cross-party criticism was the final ground, which was seen as leaving a vulnerable category of people open to divorce for something which was not their fault.

Fault was and is one of the issues which attracts most attention in the divorce debate in Northern Ireland. It was the Anglican Archbishop of Canterbury's Working Group report of 1966, *Putting Asunder*[9] which first suggested taking the fault element out of divorce, but the no-fault ethos which replaced it was most famously outlined by the English Law Commission in the same year, when it stated that:

> "the objectives of a good divorce law should be:
>
> (a) to buttress, rather than to undermine, the stability of marriage, and
>
> (b) when, regrettably, a marriage has irretrievably broken down, to enable the empty legal shell to be destroyed with the maximum of fairness, and the minimum bitterness, distress and humiliation."[10]

---

[6] Matrimonial Causes Act 1937.

[7] Attorney General for Northern Ireland, HC Debs (NI) Vol Xxii, cols 1231–1243 (1939).

[8] Matrimonial Causes Act (NI) 1939, s.2(a)–(d).

[9] SPCK, 1966.

[10] Law Comm No. 6, *Reform of the Grounds of Divorce – the Field of Choice* Cmnd 3123 (1966), para. 15.

**England – The Mixed System Rejected**

Before tracing the development of divorce in Northern Ireland any further, it is worth digressing to set out recent developments in neighbouring jurisdictions. The "mixed" system (introduced in 1973) received a mixed response in England and Wales. Ironically, it was the Law Commission who felt that:

> "one principle (fault) can serve the case of the spouse who had suffered serious offence. The other (no-fault) can serve those spouses in respect of whom no glaring misconduct can be identified and those who seek divorce against the will of a relatively innocent partner".[11]

By contrast, the Archbishop's Group predicted that a mixed system would inevitably revert to the adversarial and fault-focused ethos of the old one, and this prediction seemed to come true. The so-called "Special Procedure" introduced divorce by post to England and Wales in 1977. An administrative procedure, brought in by Rules of Court in order to save costs, it could be said to be one of the most significant factors in shaping the English divorce system. In 1994, 77% of wives' and 61% of husbands' divorces were granted on the fault facts, with adultery and behaviour being the most popular facts used.[12] This system was not free from other problems, and was roundly criticised in the review which began with the Law Commission Discussion Paper *Facing the Future*[13] in 1988. It had been the subject of a number of empirical academic studies in the 1980s and early 1990s,[14] and based on these and on their own findings, the Law Commission and the Lord Chancellor's Department, which brought forward the proposals for a new divorce law, set out a "charge sheet" of criticisms of the old law. They argued that:

1. the system did nothing to help save saveable marriages;

2. divorce could be obtained without proper consideration of the consequences and implications;

3. the system made things worse for the children;

---

[11] Para. 105.

[12] Office of Population Censuses and Surveys *Update* February 1996.

[13] Law Comm No 170 (1988).

[14] In particular see Davis and Murch, *Grounds for Divorce* (Clarendon Press), Davis, *Partisans and Mediators* (Clarendon Press, 1988), Dingwall and Eekelaar, *Divorce, Mediation and the Legal Process* (Clarendon Press, 1988).

4. the system was unjust;

5. the system was confusing, misleading and open to abuse;

6. the system was discriminatory;

7. the system distorted the parties' bargaining positions.

In essence, the divorce process was too backward-looking, too adversarial and too fast. It could be argued to be a good way to ensure that a divorce degenerated into a mudslinging pit of acrimony from which the parties and their children might never re-emerge. In the Family Law Act 1996, therefore, the English replaced their existing system with a new, purely no-fault one, designed to eliminate fault, minimise acrimony, maximise the opportunities for communication and increased understanding, and to slow the system to ensure that parties sorted out their post-divorce arrangements before the decree was issued.

Full implementation of Part II of the Family Law Act 1996, dealing with the process of divorce, has been adjourned until the full evaluations of the pilot projects on information meetings and mediation become available in 2000. Part IV of the Act, which stands alone, deals with occupation of the family home and protection from violence by non-molestation and occupation orders, and is already in force. Part II may be considered separately. The ground for divorce under the Family Law Act remains "the irretrievable breakdown of the marriage", but no particular proof of breakdown is required, except the successful completion of all stages of an extended divorce process. Under "divorce by process over time" as it is called, the process of divorce has become the ground for divorce.

The first step in initiating the process is for one or both parties to attend an information meeting where they will hear about what divorce will mean for them and their children, and about the services which are available to them. After a three month "cooling off period", one or both can then lodge a "statement of marital breakdown" with the court. This starts time running on the "period for reflection and consideration" during which time they may enter into relationship counselling with a view to saving the marriage, or take steps, through mediation, negotiation with the help of solicitors, or through court hearings, to resolve all ancillary issues. The period runs for nine months, or for fifteen if there are minor children or in certain other circumstances. At the end of the period, one or both parties lodges with the court a "statement of irretrievable marital breakdown" and a statement of the arrangements they have reached in relation to their property and children. On receipt of these documents and consideration of whether the ancillary arrangements are satisfactory, the court can pronounce a divorce order.

## Divorce in Scotland

The ground for divorce in the Divorce (Scotland) Act 1976, like that in England and Northern Ireland, is the irretrievable breakdown of marriage, proven on one of five facts, which are very similar to those in Northern Ireland. As part of the UK-wide reconsideration of the ground for divorce in the late 1980s, the Scottish Law Commission published a discussion paper[15] which recommended a move to a pure no-fault system, with irretrievable breakdown proved either by a period of notice or of separation. However, public opinion in Scotland did not support such a radical move, and many who took part in the consultation also pointed out that less radical reform could go a long way to meet the main criticisms of the existing system.

The majority of petitioners in Scotland already used the separation grounds, so the charge sheet was different to that in England. The main problem identified in Scotland was that the separation periods were too long, encouraging some abusive use of the behaviour fact by those who wanted a quick divorce, and preventing those using the separation facts from resolving property issues expeditiously. The Commission recommended reducing the two and five year periods to one and two years and abolishing desertion, which was hardly every used in proof, as a basis for divorce.[16]

These proposals have not yet been acted on in Scotland, nor has a definitive decision to retain a mixed system been taken, but the ground for divorce is again under active consideration as part of a comprehensive review of the Scottish family law system.

## Northern Ireland – The Field of Choice

Northern Ireland is currently considering the ground for divorce as part of a rolling review of family law. It is, in a sense, encouraging to

---

[15] *The Ground for Divorce – Should the Law Be Changed?* (SLC Discussion Paper No. 76, 1988).
[16] Scottish Law Commission, *Report on the reform of the ground for divorce* (SLC No. 116, 1989).

see that each of our neighbours have chosen a different way to achieve the goal of setting up a modern divorce system which meets the needs of the system users. The Republic of Ireland has taken the no-fault route, using divorce after a period of separation. In England, the new procedure of divorce by process over time has been developed. Scotland is considering retaining a mixed system.

Each of these choices was informed by an analysis of the shortcomings of the existing situation, and a knowledge of the needs of the system users. That information was not available when consideration of divorce was first mooted in Northern Ireland. A team of academics from the Queen's University of Belfast and the University of Ulster was therefore commissioned by the Office of Law Reform, the Civil Service office which has oversight of the civil law, including divorce, to carry out an empirical study of the Northern Ireland divorce system. The report, completed in December 1998, was the first to attempt to describe the system on the ground in the North – the law in the courts and solicitors' offices rather than the law in the books.[17] The research team members were Claire Archbold, Ciaran White, Pat McKee, Lynda Spence, Brendan Murtagh and Monica McWilliams. A chapter of this length cannot present the full findings of the report in addition to covering the other matters within its remit, but they inform the rest of the chapter. Therefore, the chapter will now consider the practical divorce system in the North.

## The Divorce System in Northern Ireland

On its face, the scheme of divorce established by the Matrimonial Causes (NI) Order 1978 was almost identical to that introduced in England in 1973. There are four substantive differences, which were described in debate in the Westminster Parliament as technical amendments to the original scheme. They are:

1.  There is no requirement that a solicitor certify that she has discussed reconciliation with the petitioner. It was said in Parliament that this provision had shown itself to be ineffective in England, as it merely reflected good professional practice, and was no check on the less diligent.

---

[17] The Report will be available from the Stationery Office in Belfast, entitled *Divorce in Northern Ireland – Unravelling the System* from December 1999.

2.  A social work report was until recently required in every case in which there were children.[18] Article 44 of the 1978 Order requires that there be a social worker's report in every divorce case involving children in Northern Ireland. The social worker was intended to report to the court, but also to assist with conciliation between the parents if appropriate. Not replicated in England, this provision was welcomed in Parliament as a valuable protection for the "innocent victims" of divorce but became perhaps the single biggest source of delay in the divorce system, and was abolished when the Children (NI) Order 1995 was introduced in November 1996, with no great sorrow.

3.  The oral hearing has been retained. The "Special Procedure" is not available for divorce in Northern Ireland, and the court is required[19] to hear oral evidence from the petitioner in every divorce case, whether defended or not. This fact changes the "feel" of the divorce system remarkably, and is one reason for the particular shape and character of the divorce system in the North. Although legislation has since been passed allowing the Family Rules Committee to introduce the Special Procedure,[20] their power has not yet been exercised, and in the light of subsequent developments in England, is unlikely to be.

4.  Legal aid remains freely available. The final significant difference from England is likewise procedural, as civil legal aid remains available in Northern Ireland for undefended divorce cases, and there are more generous exemptions to the Statutory Charge than are available in England and Wales.

The practitioner's overwhelming impression of family law in Northern Ireland is often how different it is to the law which he or she has been taught at University. The "book law" – the statutes and case law, as well as the English texts on them (the statutes are identical in all material regards, and so English texts are used) – give the impression of a divorce system where the decree of divorce is central, where child care and financial issues were sorted out after the divorce, and where the legal input into matrimonial breakdown is one clean slice.

---

[18] Matrimonial Causes (NI) Order 1978, Art. 44.
[19] Matrimonial Causes (NI) Order 1978, Art.3(3).
[20] Family Law (NI) Order 1993, Article 15.

That does not happen in practice. The divorce system in Northern Ireland is very different.

## What's the context? – A few vital statistics[21]

Before discussing the divorce system, it might be useful to give some idea of the social background with which we are dealing. The population of Northern Ireland in 1997 was 1,675,000. Although as in the rest of Ireland, we still have one of the youngest age structures in Europe,[22] with one quarter of the population under the age of 16, the 1997 birth rate of 14.57 per 1000 population is the lowest on record. However, the percentage of births outside marriage has risen sharply. Never rising above 6% until 1980, since then they have shown a revolutionary rise to the 1997 high of 26.6%. Sixty-four percent of these births were jointly registered by the parents. While this figure may veil a number of different situations, it certainly suggests that the 2.4% of households in the last census describing themselves as cohabiting[23] is a vast under-estimate of the non-marital families in Northern Ireland, a phenomenon which was also remarked on in the last Irish census.[24]

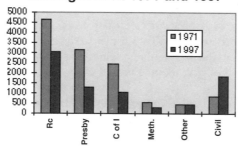

**Marriages in NI 1971 and 1997**

---

[21] Unless otherwise stated, statistics are drawn from the *Annual Reports of the Registrar General for Northern Ireland* (HMSO) and the *Northern Ireland Judicial Statistics* (Northern Ireland Court Service).

[22] P. Compton, *Demographic Review, Northern Ireland*, (Northern Ireland Economic Research Council, March 1995).

[23] *Ibid.*

[24] Drew, "Reconceptualising Families in Ireland: Changes in Demography and Family Forms"; paper presented at Queen's University of Belfast Centre for Women's Studies, January 8, 1998.

Marriage is also at its lowest ever rate in Northern Ireland, with only 4.8 marriages taking place per 1,000 of the population in 1997. Over 11% of marriages involve at least one divorcee, and between 1% and 2% a widow or widower. The average Northern Ireland groom is now 30.2 years old when he marries, the average bride is 28.2, and more and more of them are opting for a civil marriage.

These statistics help to place the legal remedy of divorce in its social context. John Haskey recently forecasted[25] that the major demographic trends in Britain in the next 25 years would be an increase in extra-marital cohabitation, an increase in the number of elderly people, and an increase in the number of women of all ages living alone. Marriage is no longer the only, or even the preferred life choice for enormous numbers of people, even in Northern Ireland, and if our legal system ignores these trends, it risks becoming irrelevant, and worse, providing no protection to people who may be in great need of it.

**Who divorces in Northern Ireland?**

Turning to divorce itself; there were 2,176 decrees nisi in 1997, a slight decrease from the previous year, but showing that numbers of divorces in the 1990s may be stabilising after the sharp rises of the 1980s. This matches trends elsewhere.[26] Although England is a high-divorce society, with a rate of 13.5 per 1,000 population in 1996, compared to Northern Ireland's 3.4 per 1,000 in that year,[27] the divorce rate in England has actually fallen and in 1997 was only the third-highest rate of divorce in Europe, after a sojourn at the top of the league.

Around two-thirds of divorce petitioners in Northern Ireland are wives, and the most frequent time for divorce is between 5 and 9 years of marriage. Unlike England and Wales, but like Scotland, a large majority of divorcing couples (79%) in Northern Ireland have minor children. One question which might be asked is whether divorce is equally divided amongst the religious denominations. In the

---

[25] During a presentation on the United Kingdom Office of National Statistics population forecasts at a conference at Staffordshire University for the Study of the Family on January 30, 1999.
[26] *Demographic Statistics* (Eurostat, Population and Social Conditions Series 3A), Table F-3.
[27] *Social Trends 28* (Office of National Statistics, 1998), Table 2.19.

1991 Census,[28] there were significantly fewer divorced or remarried Catholics than persons of other religious persuasions. There were also significantly greater numbers of divorced persons (but not such a great number of remarried persons) who stated their religious affiliation as "none". It will be interesting to see the 2001 Census on this subject.

While the number of marriages in the main Protestant denominations (Presbyterian, Church of Ireland, Methodist) resulting in divorce has remained relatively stable since 1983, the number of divorces of persons married in a Catholic ceremony, or in one of the minority Protestant denominations (such as Baptist or Brethren, who might be more likely to have moral qualms about divorce) has increased from levels well below the Northern Ireland average (in the case of the Catholic church, the annual number has doubled) to a more representative figure. This is an area in which statistics can tempt one to speculate too far, but it does seem that divorce is becoming more widely accepted among those for whom it would have been a major problem in the past. Without further data, it may be going too far to predict that the divorce rates in the denominations where it is currently rising may stabilise, as it has done in the main Protestant denominations, but it is a tempting speculation nonetheless, and observing the trend over the next few years may provide some interesting results.

### Does fault matter?

As mentioned earlier, one of the main criticisms made of the English divorce system during their reform debate was that it was adversarial, and unduly fault-focused. The Church of England (and others) have suggested that this is an inevitable feature of "mixed" divorce systems. However, the majority of divorce cases in Northern Ireland since the introduction of the 1978 Order have been based on separation rather than on the fault facts. This is similar to the experience in other jurisdictions such as Scotland and Canada.

---

[28] *Northern Ireland Census 1991, Religion Report* (HMSO 1993).

**Fact used to prove divorce 1997**

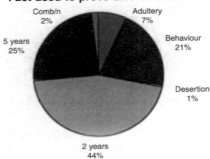

The number of petitions based on unreasonable behaviour in Northern Ireland is still a minority, but is increasing, and indicates that the preference for separation-based divorce does not necessarily place the jurisdiction in the divorce nirvana of marital dissolution without acrimony. 24.2% of High Court divorces are now based on behaviour (32.4% of wives' petitions), as are 17% of county court divorces. 77% of county court divorces are based on separation (50% on the two years and consent fact) and 61% are based on separation in the High Court (39% on the two years and consent fact). By contrast, in 1984 (when only 18.6% of cases were heard in the county court), only 14.7% of High Court divorces were based on behaviour, and 72.5% of High Court cases were based on separation, of which 46% were based on two years and consent.

This use of the no-fault facts is one of the most marked contrasts to the highly-criticised system in England. There, almost three-quarters of petitions are based on the fault facts.[29] In Scotland[30] around 65% of cases are based on the separation facts, as in Northern Ireland, but there is a marked difference between cases where there are no children, and those in which there are minor children. In the latter category, half of cases are based on behaviour. This trend is less marked in Northern Ireland. Around 26% of petitions involving children are based on behaviour, as compared to 15% of petitions where there are no children, and there is a very slightly larger proportion of adultery petitions. However, there are also almost 5% more petitions

---

[29] Office of Population Censuses and Surveys *Update* (February 1996).
[30] Scottish Law Commission Discussion Paper No. 76, *The Ground for Divorce – Should the Law be Changed?* (1988).

based on two years' separation; chosen by almost 50% of those with children. The single biggest difference between divorcing couples with and without children in Northern Ireland is that 5 years' separation is pleaded in 32% of cases without children, as compared to only 18% of cases with children.[31]

In England, the parody of unreasonable behaviour displayed in many divorce petitions was one reason for removing the fact from the statute books. Provision only of microwave TV dinners, rather than "proper dinners" such as the petitioner's mother used to make; dictatorial channel-surfing and refusal to give up the TV remote control; and persistent snoring have all featured in English divorce petitions.[32] The *Unravelling the System* team undertook a court record study of the 1990 divorce petitions in Northern Ireland, and they gave a very different picture of the behaviour of which unreasonable behaviour petitioners complain. They make grim reading. Violence is the most frequently cited, followed closely by threats of violence and verbal abuse.

The Republic of Ireland has gone down the road of pure no-fault divorce. Whether or not to retain fault is perhaps the single issue most likely to provoke hot debate in any future consultation on divorce reform in the North, because of the fear in some quarters that such a move will make divorce easier and destabilise society, and because of the deep residual commitment, both in the wider public and within the divorce-related professions, to the idea of the "innocent petitioner" whose suffering ought to be recognised by the grant of a decree based on fault.

The retention of a fault fact would require careful thought to minimise perverse incentives to those who would seek to use it in order to obtain a fast divorce, or to gain some negotiating advantage in relation to ancillary relief. There is not time to explore it here, but one might also recall the feminist argument that there are situations where accusations of fault may be the only card which an economically-less-powerful spouse holds, and that she will be entirely powerless in financial negotiation with an errant partner unless she can hold him to task for his behaviour.[33] Despite its academic interest, however, fault may well be a red herring in the debate about how best to im-

---

[31] *Unravelling the System,* figures taken from 1991 Court Record Study.

[32] *The Times,* February 19, 1996, quoted in Hoggett and Pearl, *The Family, Law and Society* (4th edn., Butterworth's, 1996), p. 217.

[33] M.A, Fineman, *The Illusion of Equality,* (University of Chicago Press, 1991).

prove the divorce system. The operation of the divorce jurisdiction in the North proves that the existence of a residual fault fact for divorce in a mixed system does not inevitably lead to a fault-based, recriminatory ethos pervading the entire system. The important factors in shaping the divorce system in the North lie elsewhere, and despite the difference in the grounds for divorce, there are strong parallels between the legal response to domestic disharmony north and south of the border, even before divorce was introduced in the latter jurisdiction.

### A long, slow matrimonial law system

One key to understanding divorce in Northern Ireland is that it is just one tool in the legal practitioner's tool kit. The team on *Unravelling the System* took a decision not to refer to "the divorce system" in Northern Ireland, but to "the matrimonial law system". Although the phrase excludes the family outside marriage, the system is largely based on remedies for married couples.[34] This is because family breakdown does not occur all of a piece. Rather, it is an incremental process; a massive emotional, mental, social and legal transition.[35] Few in Northern Ireland take the decision to divorce immediately. Divorce is the final, rather than the central act in the legal drama. For many people, the first stop is the magistrates' court, for orders relating to maintenance and child care. Recourse may be had to the Child Support Agency for child maintenance, and these steps may be taken years before the divorce actually happens.

### Before Divorce – The Legal Options

It may be useful to set out the various legal options available to couples in marital breakdown in the North. The most usual first step is a visit to the magistrates' court. This may result in an application for spousal maintenance in the domestic proceedings court,[36] commonly

---

[34] The Children (NI) Order 1996, which provides remedies in child law, and the Family Homes and Domestic Violence (NI) Order 1998, providing remedies for domestic violence, both of which provide remedies to families outside marriage on an equal basis with married couples, are the main exceptions to this rule.

[35] S. Day-Sclater, "Divorce – Coping Strategies, Conflict and Divorce Resolution"; [1998] *Family Law* 150.

[36] Domestic Proceedings (NI) Order 1980, Art 4.

known as a "separation order". The domestic proceedings court has jurisdiction to make an order for periodical payments to a spouse for any amount, and for a lump sum of up to £1,000. It does not provide a judicial separation, yet the "separation order" is perhaps the most enduring myth of Northern Irish family law. Clients want their "separation", some lawyers seem to share their confusion, and the Housing Executive in many areas requires a court order as proof of separation so that the applicant can gain rehousing priority. Before 1980, the Summary Jurisdiction (Separation and Maintenance) Act (NI) 1945 did provide for the making of a separation order by a magistrates' court;[37] although this was always of limited practical significance compared to the powers to provide for maintenance and custody of children. The domestic proceedings court also has the advantages of providing a forum to begin negotiations about full ancillary relief, and in some cases for providing an admission to adultery or behaviour which can be used in a later divorce. Some of the solicitors whom we interviewed for *Unravelling the System* also spoke of it as psychologically important for clients unwilling to take the dramatic step of obtaining a divorce, and yet needing to do something about their marriage.

Before the coming into force of the Child Support (NI) Order 1991, in April 1994, the domestic proceedings court also dealt with maintenance for children,[38] and until November 1996, with child care issues. The latter are now dealt with, in most cases, under the Children (NI) Order 1995[39] by the Family Proceedings Court, which also sits at magistrates' court level. While the domestic proceedings court is presided over by a Resident Magistrate sitting alone, family proceedings court cases are heard by a Resident Magistrate and two lay justices of the peace. These trends might be thought to have made the domestic proceedings court redundant, but the statistics suggest that it still has a role to play.

The Judicial Statistics indicate that applications for maintenance and custody under the Domestic Proceedings (Northern Ireland) Or-

---

[37] Summary Jurisdiction (Separation and Maintenance) Act (NI) 1945, s.3.
[38] The Child Support Order places an obligation on the natural parents of a child under 16, and maintenance for other categories of children for whom the Child Support Agency has no jurisdiction (Child Support (NI) Order 1991, Art 10), such as stepchildren, and older teenagers continuing in education may still be sought from the Domestic Proceedings Court.
[39] Private law applications are made under Children (NI) Order 1995, Article 8.

der 1980 were at a rate of 3,023 orders from 5,012 applications (the remainder were dismissed or withdrawn) in 1992, just before the Child Support (NI) Order 1991 came into force. In 1995, the first full year of operation of the child support legislation, 2,106 orders were made from 3,595 applications. In 1997, 1,634 orders were made from 2,764 applications. Although the domestic proceedings court is becoming less popular, therefore, it is far from redundant.

The reduction in domestic proceedings cases could be said not to represent a reduction in family breakdown, but a transfer of proceedings to the Family Proceedings Court. 1,353 applicants brought 3,616 free-standing applications under the Children Order in 1997, the first full year of its operation. 90% of these were lodged in the Family Proceedings Court, and 9% in the High Court. Only 1% were lodged with Family Care Centres. 81% of these applications were in relation to private law matters. Contact was the subject matter of 37% of applications, and residence 29%. Only 9% of cases were care proceedings. Almost half of the applications were brought by fathers, and a quarter by mothers. Grandparents brought a small percentage of applications, and 3 applications were brought by children. The most striking thing about these statistics is that, as the Children Order Advisory Committee point out in their First Report, the Children Order is in practice a private law piece of legislation.

What of those who have more significant assets than can be dealt with in the domestic proceedings court? For them too, divorce is unlikely to be the first step in the legal process. There are very few ancillary relief orders made either by consent or after a hearing in Northern Ireland, and it seems too simplistic to say that this is because the population has insignificant property. In the court record study undertaken for *Unravelling the System* 73% of divorce petitions referred to a previous court order; almost exclusively obtained from the domestic proceedings court. The average magistrates' court order was obtained just under nine years after marriage, and an average of just over four years before divorce proceedings were issued. Those solicitors whom we interviewed spoke of a significant number of cases in which a private separation agreement was drawn up and signed before divorce proceedings were commenced, or even perhaps contemplated. This was rarely an alternative to divorce; the precedents which most practitioners use include a provision (of dubious enforceability) whereby one party undertakes to petition for divorce after two years, and the other undertakes not to withhold their consent. Perhaps the biggest unresolved question of *Unravelling the Sys-*

*tem* was what became of these agreements – the court record study revealed very few prior agreements recorded in the petition, and although most ancillary relief orders were made by consent, they occurred in only around one in seven cases. One possibility is that agreements which were fully performed by the time of the divorce were not recorded in the petition, and that there was no need to have them converted into court orders. However, some element of mystery remains.

### The matrimonial law system in Northern Ireland

So far, this chapter has tried to paint a picture of what actually happens in Northern Ireland when a marriage breaks down. This process may be summarised by presenting it as a "real world" narrative of a woman whose marriage is in difficulty. She doesn't start by rushing off to the divorce court. She is most likely to get legal advice, to go to the domestic proceedings court for her "separation order". This may give her maintenance. Even if the order is nominal, it is a passport to reallocated housing. If she has children, she may apply to the Child Support Agency at this stage, and is likely to either obtain a family proceedings court order or enter into negotiation with her husband about their child care arrangements. She is unlikely (whether because she is not "ready" psychologically, or because there is no reason save remarriage to do so) to bring divorce proceedings immediately. When she does so, she is likely to use a separation fact. The divorce process in Northern Ireland is slow and separation-based in the majority of cases.

### An undertow of violence

What I have not yet mentioned is the undertow of violence and acrimony which is evident not only in the high percentage of violence allegations in unreasonable behaviour cases, but also in the number of personal protection and exclusion orders obtained in the magistrates' courts. A total of 6,494 protective orders were made in Northern Ireland in 1997. Of these, just over 2,200 were interim personal protection orders, and around the same number were interim exclusion orders. There were just over 2,000 applications, for full personal protection orders, and around the same for exclusion orders, but just under half of each of these were withdrawn (945 personal protection, 953 exclusion). Therefore, slightly under 1,000 of each order were actually made; around half by consent. This reflects the position in relation to barring applications in the South, and is worrying, in that it is not clear what happens when an application is withdrawn. It may be because the parties have reconciled after a one-off incident of violence which is unlikely to be repeated, because a vexatious application has been withdrawn, because the applicant has taken the abuser back after promises that he will not beat her again, or, most worryingly, because she has been intimidated out of continuing proceedings.

The new Family Homes and Domestic Violence (NI) Order 1998 replaces the personal protection and exclusion order with non-molestation and occupation orders, available to a wider range of family members, including elderly parents, former spouses, gay couples, and anyone "living as a member of the same household other than as lodger and tenant".[40] If a non-molestation order has been made, a court which subsequently determines any application for residence or contact with a child by the respondent must take into account in deciding whether to make the order the risk of harm to the child from seeing or hearing any violence by the respondent against any other person.[41] The new law comes into force at a time when the agencies working to stamp out domestic violence in Northern Ireland are building a base from which to deliver an integrated, effective service. The Regional Forum on Domestic Violence has a membership drawn from the public, private and voluntary sectors, as well as the churches. Several pilot projects developing an integrated agency response are getting underway at the moment. Again, it would be fascinating to discuss these initiatives, and the initiatives which are being implemented in the South arising from the Report of the Task Force on Violence Against Women, but this is beyond the scope of this book.[42]

**The matrimonial law system, north and south**

The matrimonial law systems north and south, even before divorce was introduced in the Republic, show some clear similarities. The operation of the matrimonial law system in the South before divorce

---

[40] Family Homes and Domestic Violence (NI) Order 1998, Art. 3.
[41] *Ibid.;* Art 28.
[42] R. Horgan, "Domestic Violence – A Case for Reform" (1998) 1 I.J.F.L. 3–6.

became available was mapped by Fahey and Lyons in 1995.[43] Although their methodology was different to that in *Unravelling the System,* parallels emerge. Lawyer-negotiated settlements are common among the better-off. Among the less well off, orders from the lower courts are the main form of remedy on breakdown. Both jurisdictions at that point in time shared a long, non-precipitate matrimonial breakdown process which stands in stark contrast to the precipitate divorce process in England and Wales. More worryingly, a high rate of domestic violence seems to lurk beneath the surface of both systems.[44]

## LOOKING TO THE FUTURE – THE SHAPE OF THINGS TO COME

### Post-Divorce Arrangements – Child Care

As I have said, the majority of divorcing couples in Northern Ireland tend to regulate their child care issues early – when they separate rather than when they divorce. 73% of couples in *Unravelling the System's* court record survey had a previous court order; 86% of couples with children as compared to 47% of those without. The records date from before the Child Support Agency, which commenced operation in 1994, and the Children (NI) Order 1995. Thus, the orders obtained might be in relation to custody, maintenance or both. The court record study also gave a good indication of patterns of post-divorce child care arrangements, with most divorce court custody or access orders being confirmatory of an earlier magistrates' court order. 88% of custody orders were in favour of the mother, and only 11.5% in favour of the father. Joint or split custody found little favour in pre-Children Order Northern Ireland. The compulsory social work reports in the Court Record Study indicated that at the point just before the divorce hearing when the social worker reported, 26% of absent parents had little or no contact with their children.

The social work report mentioned above was welcomed when it was introduced in the 1978 Order. Article 44 required that in every divorce case involving minor children, a Welfare Report was to be

---

[43] T. Fahey and M. Lyons, *Matrimonial breakdown and Family Law in Ireland: A Sociological Study* (Oak Tree Press, 1995).

[44] See further C. White and C. Archbold, "Looking North, Looking South; Comparing legal responses to matrimonial breakdown in the two jurisdictions" (1998) 1 I.J.F.L. 20–22.

made by a social worker. Without this report, the judge could not make the declaration required by the legislation, that the arrangements for the children were "satisfactory or the best that can be arranged in the circumstances". The social worker's role was both to report to the court on the state of the arrangements, and to help the parents come to a mediated agreement if they could not do so unaided. In practice, the work was given to already over-stretched local Area Child Protection Units, and it is unsurprising that 'routine' divorce cases were given a lower priority than emergency protection work, causing delays of six months and more in making the report. However, even without the delay, the social workers found themselves providing a service that was usually not needed; reporting on stable arrangements which had often been in place for several years.

### A holistic approach to family breakdown

The Welfare Report system targeted help too late in the marital breakdown process, and was not given separate resources. However, Welfare Reports did not fail because of the nature of the intervention. Indeed, they could be seen as an early attempt to provide an element of interprofessional working together, and to deliver a holistic package of remedies to those suffering family breakdown. This holistic approach; involving working together by legal professionals, social workers, counsellors, mediators and others, is a common feature of family law systems in the late twentieth century. In Canada, Australia and New Zealand the approach is delivered through the specially designated "Family Court", and the innovative and exciting approaches of these jurisdictions have inspired many people from elsewhere, although the funding problems of such a high-input system have recently begun to hit the headlines in Australia.

However, the realisation that family breakdown is not a purely legal phenomenon is not limited to jurisdictions with a specially-designated family court. The concept of working together is integral to the Children (NI) Order 1995, as to the Children Act 1989 in England. In that jurisdiction, the idea of the holistic approach was forcefully expressed twenty-five years ago in the Finer Report.[45] It can be seen in the Family Law Act provision for information meetings about

---

[45] Finer et al; *Report of the Committee on One Parent Families* (Cmnd 5629, 1974).

divorce, and the provision that before legal aid for legal advice on divorce is granted, the parties must attend a meeting to find out about whether mediation would be appropriate for them.[46]

The approach is further developed in the Labour Government Interdepartmental consultation document *Supporting Families*.[47] The document attempts to develop the ways in which social policies strengthen and protect families across the board, dealing with advice and services, financial support, balancing work and home, strengthening marriage and better supporting "serious family problems". It prioritises parenthood rather than partnership, and tries to emphasise that "while marriage provides the most reliable framework for raising children, . . . [yet] there are strong and mutually supportive families outside marriage".[48] The document is ambitious and relevant to a range of areas. However, one strong theme is its emphasis on support and education before and during family crisis rather than legal intervention afterwards. The paper does not pretend that the legal system is the main way of supporting families, and emphasises that children are raised by families and not by government – the aim of government should be the role of "best supporting actor".[49] Support is targeted through a number of media – a new National Family and Parenting Institute, a National Parenting Helpline and an enhanced role for Health Visitors are three examples. Education and information are prescribed for those entering marriage, and at all stages of parenthood, as well as in combatting teen pregnancy and domestic violence.

It is worth mentioning two of the paper's responses to the increase in numbers of the family outside marriage. It suggests a civil "naming ceremony" for babies; which may be a good way to encourage responsible parenting. If it were to prove popular, it would provide a marked contrast to the extremely low take-up at present of Children Act parental responsibility agreements for unmarried fathers[50]; the mechanism by which an unmarried father can acquire a

---

[46] Family Law Act s.29.

[47] Available at http://www.homeoffice.gov.uk/.

[48] Para. 4.5.

[49] Barton, "Spending more time with their families – the Government's consultation document"; [1999] *Family Law* 136.

[50] Children Act 1989, s.4, Children (NI) Order 1995, Art 7. So far in Northern Ireland there have, to the author's knowledge, been no parental responsibility agreements.

recognised legal role in his child's life. In this regard, it might also be of interest to mention that it is proposed to give automatic parental responsibility to all unmarried fathers in England whose names are jointly registered on the birth certificate. Options relating to unmarried fathers and parental responsiblity, whether automatic joint parental responsibility, joint parental responsibility on joint registration or the improvement of information about parental responsibility agreements to parents who jointly register a birth is the subject of a Government consultation paper in Northern Ireland at present, and it will be interesting to see the outcome of consultation.[51]

Northern Ireland divorce professionals have taken well to working together under the Children Order, and many now recognise the importance of non-legal interventions. However, mediation has yet to become widely-used. There is still great misunderstanding of it among professionals and potential clients alike, with many believing it to be a form of reconciliation counselling. Under 100 couples undertook mediation last year with the Northern Ireland Family Mediation Service; the service provider in the North. One important question facing divorce professionals in the North is how to encourage those for whom mediation would be appropriate to try it. Another is how to improve people's knowledge and understanding of their rights and responsibilities towards other family members. The information meetings being piloted in England, as well as the parent education programmes, helplines and information provision suggested in *Supporting Families* are another area in which a little development could have a big impact.

In short, therefore, another way in which the matrimonial law system in Northern Ireland, like that in the Republic, is changing most rapidly is in the recognition of the importance of freely-chosen non-legal interventions in helping families in breakdown and those under stress. In the North, mediation professionals see a rapid development of mediation occurring in the South, and this is an area in which working together across the border is very possible, and in which enhanced co-operation could be of great benefit.

---

[51] Office of Law Reform, *Parental Responsibility for Unmarried Fathers: Court Procedures for the Determination of Paternity* (July 1999).

**Post-Divorce Arrangements – Finance**

As discussed above, financial arrangements in Northern Ireland are in practice often made before divorce, although full ancillary relief is only available afterwards. *Unravelling the System* found that 86% of couples who began divorce proceedings in 1997 were living separately at the time the petition was lodged. Practice in financial provision cases takes place on a very case-by-case basis in the north. Few cases are contested, and there are fewer reported decisions. One major difference between the two jurisdictions is in relation to the goal of financial provision. While provision in the Republic has an effective presumption of ongoing support, provision on divorce in the North requires a judge to ask whether a clean break between the parties is desirable. A clean break is not to be sought where there are children, or where a wife has not worked for so long that she will be unable to find a suitable job. However, in many other cases where the couple have some assets, much financial negotiation takes place around an attempt to find a lump sum which will "buy out" maintenance, allowing the parties to have nothing further to do with each other. This difference in the two systems is significant, but even given it, there are other areas relating to financial provision in which recent developments are of interest and relevance.

The nature of family assets is changing and becoming more complex, and patterns of earning within the family are changing dramatically. There has been debate in both England and Northern Ireland in recent years as to whether to move from a system of almost absolute judicial discretion in making financial and property orders on divorce, to one which is more easily understandable and predictable by a layperson. At present, periodical payments, lump sum and property adjustment orders are available from the court, which will make a decision taking into account a wide variety of factors unconstrained by mathematical formulae or pre-ordained proportionate division.[52]

**Procedural Reform in Ancillary Relief**

The most recent innovations in Northern Ireland have been the active case management techniques introduced by several divorce county courts, and at the High Court in Belfast. These include directions hearings and regular relisting of cases to prevent drift and encourage

---

[52] Matrimonial Causes (NI) Order 1978, Arts 25, 26.

opportunities for negotiation. They are similar but unrelated to the innovations introduced by the Ancillary Relief Pilot Projects in England and Wales,[53] which are a smaller-scale study of the sort of increased judicial case management, streamlining and cost-efficiency techniques envisaged for civil cases by the Woolf Report[54] and under consideration in the Civil Justice Review for Northern Ireland.[55]

### Substantive Reform of Ancillary Relief

In England, the ancillary relief pilot projects were taken forward under the supervision of the Ancillary Relief Working Party. An Ancillary Relief Advisory Group drawn from this was in 1998 asked to report on possible reforms to the law relating to financial provision on divorce. As discussed above, financial provision on divorce in Northern Ireland, as in England and Wales, is made on the basis of judicial discretion, taking into account a wide range of factors, including the desirability of a "clean break". The system had been criticised as being very uncertain. Although the orders made might be predictable to lawyers, they were not to lay people. This, it is claimed, makes all-issues mediation particularly difficult, as couples have no real idea what a court might award were they to take a different route. The complexity of the system was such as to value individual justice over certainty. However, it could also be argued that the weighting towards a clean break was a factor in the poverty trap in which many women found themselves in after divorce. The Advisory Group's terms of reference were "to advise the Lord Chancellor on all aspects of ancillary relief, including any issues which may arise concerning the substantive law". The Lord Chancellor asked the group to consider three issues in particular:[56]

1.  Whether, subject to the interests of the children (which would be given first priority) and to any prior agreement by the parties, there should be a presumption that property gained during the marriage should be divided 50/50 between the parties.

2.  Whether, subject to safeguards, pre– (and/or post–) nuptial agreements should be legally binding.

---

[53] Details available at http://www.open.gov.uk/lcd/psintint.html. See also Thorpe LJ, "Procedural Reform in Ancillary Relief"; [1996] *Family Law* 356.
[54] Available online by search from http://www.open.gov.uk.
[55] Not yet published (at the time of writing).
[56] [1998] *Family Law* 381.

3.  Whether the modified equal division of matrimonial property[57] in Scotland was an appropriate model for the way forward.

The Advisory Group were unanimously opposed to the introduction of a presumptive equal division, and did not think the Scottish system was appropriate for England. However, they were divided as to whether the status quo should be retained, or whether the principles on which judges make financial orders should be codified.[58]

Despite this result, the Government Consultation Paper *Supporting Families,* discussed above, came out in favour of both prenuptial agreements and a presumption of equal division of property on divorce. The paper suggested safeguards to protect economically weaker spouses and children, in that an agreement would not be legally enforceable:

1.  if there were children,

2.  if it would be unenforceable under the general law of contract, for example where an attempt was made to place an obligation on a third party without their advance agreement;

3.  where one or both parties had not received independent legal advice;

4.  where the court considered that enforcing the agreement would cause significant injustice to either party or to a child of the marriage;

5.  where there had not been full disclosure of assets;

6.  where the arrangement was made fewer than 21 days before the marriage.

The Consultation Paper also considered how to increase certainty and clarity in the law of financial provision on divorce, and mentioned that the Government is considering adding an overarching objective to the law. This objective, to do that which is fair and reasonable between the parties and any child of the family, together with a set of guiding principles, would be designed to make clear the process currently followed by judges in allocating property on divorce. The principles proposed are:

---

[57] Family Law (Scotland) Act 1985, ss.9–11.
[58] See "Ancillary Relief Reform" [1998] *Family Law* 576.

1. to promote the welfare of the children, including the housing needs of the parents as primary and secondary carers;

2. to take into account any written agreement reached before or during marriage, but not enforced because one or more of the safeguards had not been met;

3. to divide any surplus to achieve a fair result, recognising that fairness will usually require an equal distribution of the assets; and

4. to try to terminate the financial relationships between the parties at the earliest practicable date.[59]

It remains to be seen whether this reform will be enacted. There is not the same groundswell of professional and academic opinion in favour of change as there was at the time of the last reform of ancillary relief in the early 1980s, and it could be that the English process will survive in its present form for some time, subject to the procedural reforms being piloted around the country. Consideration of ancillary relief will be on the agenda as part of Northern Ireland's rolling review of family law, and will involve consideration of developments among all our neighbours.

## The Pensions Conundrum

The final issue which this chapter will touch on is possibly the one which gives family practitioners the biggest headaches in practice – advising divorcing couples with private or occupational pensions. The valuation of volatile future assets is one problem; another is that until recently, the courts in Northern Ireland had no powers to make orders affecting assets held by third parties such as pension fund managers.

The significance of pension assets became evident in the 1980s, with the popularisation of private pension provision. As a pension might be the largest asset owned by a divorcing couple, who might not own sufficient other property to compensate the non-fund-member spouse for loss of pension rights, it was imperative that the courts began to find ways of dealing with the issue. Adjourning decisions on financial provision, or making deferred orders payable only when

---

[59] See "Ancillary Relief Again" [1998] *Family Law* 721 at 781–782.

the pension lump sum became available were always unpopular moves; as without a judicial crystal ball, such decisions were inevitably "hostages to fortune". However, they were occasionally made,[60] despite judicial reluctance to defer a decision indefinitely. Such orders were therefore more probable where the pension was likely to crystallise in the near future.

In a divorce based on five years' separation, where the non-compensatable loss to the respondent will result in "grave financial hardship", the grant of a decree nisi can be refused[61] and, in a case based on two years' separation with consent or five years' separation, the decree absolute may be delayed if appropriate financial provision has not been made for the respondent.[62] The former power has been invoked in England in relation to pensions.[63] The pensions problem may also be one reason for the remarkable increase in judicial separation petitions in Northern Ireland over the past five years. From around 20 petitions a year in the 1980s, resulting in around 15 decrees, there are now almost one hundred petitions a year, almost all brought by wives although the number of decrees issued has increased only slightly. It is hypothesised that a judicial separation petition is sometime issued as a negotiation tool, and when satisfactory compensation for loss of pension rights is reached, the petition is withdrawn and a fresh divorce petition issued.

It was *Brooks v. Brooks*[64] which really ignited professional and public interest in the pensions issue in 1995. Although the recommendations of the Pensions Management Institute Report *Pensions and Divorce* (May 1993), including both earmarking and pension sharing had not yet been effected in legislation, the judge in *Brooks* was able to split the pension fund by an imaginative use of the property adjustment order,[65] and her decision, on the unusual facts, was upheld in its essence by both the Court of Appeal and House of Lords, along with heavy hints that Parliamentary action was necessary.

The first stage of this action came with the court power to "ear-

---

[60] *Legrove v. Legrove* [1994] 2 F.L.R. 119, *Hughes v. Hughes* (unreported, NI Family Division, Girvan J, December 4, 1995), *Crozier v. Crozier* (1994) 1 F.L.R. 126.

[61] Matrimonial Causes (NI) Order 1978, Art 7.

[62] Matrimonial Causes (NI) Order 1978, Art 12.

[63] *Julian v. Julian* (1972) 117 Sol. J. 616, see also *McReynolds v. McReynolds*, unreported judgement of Lord Lowry, Northern Ireland, May 12, 1987.

[64] [1996] 1 A.C. 375.

[65] Matrimonial Causes (NI) Order 1978, Art 26.

mark" pensions in Article 168 of the Pensions (NI) Order 1996. Although revolutionary in allowing the court to make orders binding on fund trustees, the power is of limited use, and proposals on pension splitting; using some of the accumulated pension capital to allow the non-fund member to make her own pension provision (either within or outside the scheme) are being developed into legislation. In this regard, the pension-splitting powers[66] in the South, which are already in operation, are ahead of those in the North.

The DSS paper *Pension-sharing on Divorce: reforming pensions for a fairer future*[67] sets out the way in which pension-sharing will be achieved in the United Kingdom. Importantly, it will apply only to divorce proceedings beginning "after the implementation of the policy", and is not retrospective. It involves private and occupational schemes, and also SERPS contributions, but not the basic State pension, as it is already possible to substitute a former spouse's contribution record for one's own following divorce. Pension-sharing will be available as part of a court order, or as part of a consent order based on agreement between the parties. The paper sets out the detail of how pension-sharing will work in individual cases, how information is to be gleaned and how fund managers and trustees are to be notified of proceedings. The reform is being carried out UK-wide, and a version of it will apply to Northern Ireland.

## CONCLUSION

It is hoped that this brief overview will help to set discussion of the divorce system in the Republic in a wider context. Family law is an area in which discussion and comparison can be very fruitful – if in the widest international sense, then certainly where two neighbouring systems in practice share so many similarities. Reform of pension provision on divorce, and of protection from domestic violence, are recent initiatives which have involved action in both Belfast and Dublin, and the provision of mediation, information and other support services for families under stress is another area in which huge strides have recently been made in both jurisdictions.

In relation to divorce itself, the subject of this book, the first thing to say is that it is not a stand-alone remedy; it cannot be separated

---

[66] Family Law Act 1995, s12, Family Law (Divorce) Act 1996, s.17.
[67] DSS June 1998.

from its context within the wider family law system. The ground for divorce itself may be relatively unimportant, but what is significant is that the family law system should provide appropriate and timely legal interventions, along with other forms of support, to families under stress at the time at which they are needed. Where the system in Northern Ireland has succeeded, it has done this. Where it has failed, as with the social work welfare reports, it has been because help was unavailable when it was needed, and was offered at too late a stage. The ending of a marriage in both jurisdictions in Ireland is not something which is entered into lightly, and the services offered must recognise that it can be a long process.

In the South, divorce was introduced for the first time in 1997. In England and Wales, root and branch reform was enacted in 1996. Scotland is currently considering whether to go down the no-fault path, or to develop the law in its own way. The research which has been undertaken in Northern Ireland shows clearly that people in that jurisdiction divorce differently from those in England. When the research is published, and in any subsequent government discussion papers and public consultation on divorce, it is hoped that there will be a wide debate about what divorce system will best meet the needs of the people of Northern Ireland. That debate is likely to include not only discussion of the ground for divorce, but also of ways to develop a more holistic approach to family breakdown. And this may be an area in which, for law reformers in the two jurisdictions of Ireland, as well as for couples using the system, dialogue can bring many benefits.

# Chapter 4

# Tax Implications of Divorce

## *Hilary Walpole\**

## INTRODUCTION

Marital breakdown is a common occurrence. In Ireland, when dealing with marital breakdown, married couples have to confront many complex legal, financial and emotional issues in an effort to achieve a satisfactory resolution to their marriage breakdown. These issues include questions of maintenance, division of assets, custody of and access to children, succession rights, pension entitlements, occupation of the family home. Some of these issues may have tax implications.

The statutory references have been abbreviated for this chapter as follows:

| | |
|---|---|
| Taxes Consolidation Act 1997 | – TCA 1997 |
| Finance Act | – F. Act |
| Family Law (Divorce) Act 1996 | – FL (D)A 1996 |
| Social Welfare (Consolidation) Act 1993 | – SW (Con) Act 1993 |

### Tax Advantages

A valid marriage ceremony recognised by Irish law attracts certain tax advantages not available to any other kind of relationship. To appreciate how marriage breakdown brings about certain changes from a tax point of view, it is helpful if one has a basic understanding of the tax implications pertaining to the marital status. This chapter deals with the salient tax issues of marriage followed by a consideration of the tax implications at the different stages of marital breakdown with particular reference to maintenance and transfer of assets.

---

*\* Hilary Walpole is a director in PricewaterhouseCoopers. She is the author of* Tax Implications of Marital Breakdown.

# 1. INCOME

## 1.1 INCOME TAX

### 1.1.1 Husband and wife living together

A marriage ceremony of itself does not give rise to any income tax advantage. To obtain any income tax benefits, a couple must be legally married and "living together".

Under the income tax rules a married couple are "living together" unless either:

> "(a) they are separated under an order of a Court of competent jurisdiction or by deed of separation, or
>
> (b) they are in fact separated in such circumstances that the separation is likely to be permanent."[1]

Accordingly, it is assumed that a married couple are living together unless there is a definite separation, either by court order or as a matter of fact.

The advantages obtained by a married couple living together include:

(1) entitlement to married allowance (double the single persons allowance)[2];

(2) entitlement to double the single person's tax bands[3];

(3) entitlement to be assessed jointly, separately or as single people.[4]

### 1.1.2 Joint Assessment

Joint assessment is not available for the tax year in which the marriage takes place and each spouse must be assessed as a single person.[5] Joint assessment may apply for the second year of marriage either by actual election or deemed election.[6]

---

[1]  S. 1015(2) TCA 1997.
[2]  S. 461 TCA 1997.
[3]  S. 15 TCA 1997.
[4]  S. 1015–1024 TCA 1997.
[5]  S. 1020 TCA 1997.
[6]  S. 1018 (1), (2) and (4) TCA 1997.

Either election may be withdrawn by either spouse before the end of the tax year. This must be done in writing.[7]

When special provisions for married couples were introduced in the Finance Act 1980, it was enacted that the husband was assessable in respect of his own and his wife's total income and liable to pay any tax due on their joint incomes subject to certain exceptions.[8] A return of income would be submitted by the husband showing his own and his wife's income. He was granted the allowances and reliefs which a married couple was entitled to. Since April 6, 1994, a wife can also be the assessable spouse.[9]

## Example

Tax Bill for 1999/2000 for a married couple living together and earning income as follows:

|  | IR£ |
|---|---|
| Higher Income spouse | 30,000 |
| Lower Income spouse | 5,000 |
| Total and Taxable Income | 35,000 |
|  |  |
| 28,000 at 24% | 6,720 |
| 7,000 at 46% | 3,220 |
| 35,000 | 9,940 |
| Less: Personal Allowance (£8,400 at 24%) | (2,016) |
|  | 7,924 |
|  |  |
| Total tax due on joint assessment basis | 7,924 |

In order to claim joint assessment, it is not necessary for both spouses to have income. Therefore, joint assessment may be claimed if income accrues to the husband only or wife only.

## 1.1.3 Separate assessment

Separate assessment only applies where a married couple have elected

---

7 S. 1018(3)TCA 1997.
8 S. 1017 TCA 1997.
9 S. 1019 (2)(a)TCA 1997.

for or are deemed to have elected for joint assessment and a special application for separate assessment is made.[10]

Under separate assessment, income tax is assessed, charged and recovered from each spouse as if they were not married. Where either a husband or wife elects for separate assessment, they can retain the tax savings, if any, of joint assessment and at the same time have their income tax assessments and returns of income dealt with separately.[11] The personal allowances and reliefs available to both husband and wife are the same as in the case of joint assessment. In addition, the total tax payable cannot exceed the amount due if an election for separate assessment had not been made.

Any unused balances of allowances, reliefs and rate bands of one spouse are allocated against the income of the other spouse. The aggregate liability is exactly the same as under joint assessment.[12]

**Example**

Tax Bill for 1999/2000 for a married couple living together and earning income as follows:

|  | IR£ |
|---|---|
| Higher Income spouse | 30,000 |
| Lower Income spouse | 5,000 |

|  | Higher income spouse's Tax Bill IR£ | | Lower income spouse's Tax Bill IR£ | |
|---|---|---|---|---|
| Total and Taxable Income | 35,000 | | 5,000 | |
| 14,000 at 24% | 3,360 | 5,000 at 24% | 1,200 | |
| 9,000 at 24% | 2,160 | | | |
| 7,000 at 46% | 3,200 | | | |
| 35,000 | 8,740 | | 1,200 | |
| Less: Personal Allowance (4,200 at 24%) | (1,008) | (4,200 at 24%) | (1,008) | |
|  | 7,732 | | 192 | 7,924 |

[10] S. 1023 TCA 1997.
[11] S. 1023(2) TCA 1997.
[12] S. 1024(3) and (4) TCA 1997.

The aggregate liability is exactly the same as under joint assessment. The example shows that the unutilised 24%    tax rate band of the lower income spouse is transferred to the higher income spouse.

### 1.1.4  Single Assessment

Where a married couple are living together income tax is assessed on each spouse as if they were not married unless an election is made or deemed to have been made to have their incomes jointly assessed for tax.[13] If such a notice is given to the Revenue, the spouses will be assessed as single persons until such time as the election is withdrawn by the spouse who made it.[14] It is important to note, therefore, that deliberate action must be taken by either party to a marriage if they wish to be taxed under the single assessment basis.

Since both spouses are effectively treated as single persons there is no provision whereby one spouse may transfer any balance of unused allowances or tax rate bands to the other spouse. The benefit of the unused allowances may therefore be lost and for this reason single assessment is generally less advantageous than joint assessment.

### Example

Tax Bill for 1999/2000 for a married couple living together and earning income as follows:

|  | IR£ |
|---|---|
| Higher Income spouse | 30,000 |
| Lower Income spouse | 5,000 |

|  | Higher income spouse's Tax Bill IR£ |  | Lower income spouse's Tax Bill IR£ |
|---|---|---|---|
| Total and Taxable Income | 35,000 |  | 5,000 |
| 14,000 at 24% | 3,360 | 5,000 at 24% | 1,200 |
| 16,000 at 24% | 7,360 |  |  |
| 30,000 | 10,720 |  | 1,200 |

[13] S. 1016 TCA 1997.
[14] S. 1018 TCA 1997.

Less: Personal Allowance

| | | | | | |
|---|---|---|---|---|---|
| (4,200 at 24%) | (1,008) | (4,200 at 24%) | (1,008) | | |
| | 9,712 | | 192 | 9,904 | |

A comparison of the tax bills arising on the various assessment options shows:

| | |
|---|---|
| Joint Assessment (Para 1.1.2) | 7,924 |
| Separate Assessment (Para 1.1.3) | 7,924 |
| Single Assessment (Para 1.1.4) | 9,904 |

By choosing single assessment, the married couple have an increased tax bill of IR£1,980.

## 1.2 PAY RELATED SOCIAL INSURANCE (PRSI) AND HEALTH CONTRIBUTION LEVY (HCL)

Although PRSI and levies do not form part of the tax legislation, they are considered by the layman to be another form of taxation, as in most cases, PRSI and the health contribution levy are payable at the same time as income tax.

Marital status does not affect liability to PRSI and levies as these depend solely on the reckonable income of particular individuals. Therefore, a married couple are treated separately for determining a PRSI or health contribution levy liability, if any.

In the case of self employed individuals where joint assessment applies, the assessable spouse is liable from a collection point of view for any unpaid PRSI and HCL due by the non assessable spouse subject to the right of the revenue to seek payment from the non assessable spouse if his/her liability remains unpaid.[15]

Therefore, it follows that if either separate or single assessment applies, there is no question of one spouse being liable to discharge his/her spouse's unpaid PRSI or levies liability.

---

[15] S. 20(3) SW (Con.) Act 1993; Health Contributions (Amendment) Regs. 1988, Art 3.

## 2. MAINTENANCE

### 2.1 FACTUAL SEPARATION

When a married couple decide to separate or live apart, one of the first tax consequences to arise is the change in their income tax status.

Both formal and informal separations are recognised for income tax purposes. It has been recognised by case law that not all couples living apart are necessarily separated. A separation may be due to business travel, illness, etc of one of the spouses. There must be an intention by the parties to end the marriage. Therefore, couples living apart due to circumstances beyond their control are normally regarded for income tax purposes as living together. For example, in a 1947 High Court decision, it was held that the wife was "living with" her husband where he, a Garda, was compelled to live at least thirty miles from her licensed premises (*D Ua Clothasaigh v. Patrick McCartan*[16]).

Examples of likely permanent separation could include one spouse leaving the marital home to live with a third party, living of separate lives but remaining under the same roof, etc.

This phrase "living apart" has been recently considered in the UK. In *Holmes v. Mitchell*[17] it was held that the Commissioners were entitled to find that a couple who lived as separate households under the same roof were permanently separated for tax purposes. Following this case, the UK Revenue issued guidelines for similar cases. In particular, a UK inspector is instructed to ask questions along the following lines:

(1) How has the house been divided up and what are the arrangements for using kitchen and bathroom facilities?

(2) What services do they provide for each other, for example, meals, laundry, etc?

(3) What financial arrangements have been made in relation to the alleged separation?

(4) How do they manage to avoid each other?

---

[16] Vol. 2 I.T.C. 237.
[17] [1991] S. T.C. 25.

It is likely that an Irish inspector would ask similar questions in order to reach a conclusion.

There have been no recent reported Irish tax cases on "living together".

It would appear reasonably clear that a couple can be living together in the same household even when they are not sleeping in the same bed and where their motivation is simply to stay together for the good of the children. If a husband lives in the same house as his wife, but only as a lodger and his wife is living in adultery with another man in the house, the spouses are not "living with each other in the same household".

### 2.1.1 Tax year of separation – separation likely to be permanent

In the year of separation, the couple is living together for part of the year and separated for the remainder. A question needs to be asked. Do the income tax rules for married couples or separated couples apply in the tax year of separation?

### Joint Assessment

An assessable spouse is entitled to the married allowance if the couple is taxed on the joint assessment basis.[18] There is no provision in the Taxes Consolidation Act 1997 for apportioning allowances on a time basis. If a married allowance is due, it is due for the entire year.

The assessable spouse is liable to income tax for that tax year on his/her own income for the full year and on the spouse's income up to the date of separation.

The non-assessable spouse is taxed on his/her own income from the date of separation to the end of that tax year and is entitled to the single person's allowance and single rate tax bands.

---

[18] S. 461(a) TCA 1997.

**Example**

Date of Factual Separation: July 5, 1999

Tax Bill for 1999/2000 for a couple earning income as follows:

|                                                          |         | IR£    |
| -------------------------------------------------------- | ------- | ------ |
| Assessable spouse                                        |         | 30,000 |
| Non-Assessable spouse – Up to July 5, 1999               |         | 1,250  |
|                        July 6, 1999 – April 5, 2000      |         | 3,750  |
|                                                          |         | 5,000  |

|                                        | Assessable spouse's Tax Bill IR£ |                  | Non-Assessable spouse's Tax Bill IR£ |        |
| -------------------------------------- | -------- | ---------------- | ------- | ------ |
| Total and Taxable Income (s)           | 35,000   |                  | 3,750   |        |
|                            (w)         | 1,250    |                  |         |        |
|                                        | 31,250   |                  | 3,750   |        |
| 28,000 at 24%                          | 6,720    | 3,750 at 24%     | 900     |        |
| 3,250 at 46%                           | 1,495    |                  |         |        |
| 31,250                                 | 8,215    |                  | 900     |        |
| Less: Personal Allowance (£8,400 at 24%) | (2,016) | (3,750 at 24%)   | (900)   |        |
|                                        | 6,199   (1) |               | nil     | 6,199  |
| After tax income (own only)            | 23,801   |                  | 5,000   |        |
| Net disposable income                  | 23,081   (2) |              | 5,000   |        |

(1) Personal Allowances limited to income taxable at the 24% rate.
(2) £30,000 – £6,199 = £23,801.

The married couple's tax bill of IR£6,199 in the tax year of separation is less than for a married couple living together (para. 1.1.2).

   In this example, the wife's income has been apportioned on a time basis over the tax year. In practice, arbitrary apportionments cannot be made. Actual details of the wife's income from April 6 to date of separation and date of separation to the following 5 April must be obtained.

**Separate Assessment**

As for joint assessment, this remains in force for the tax year of separation. However, transfers of tax free allowances and tax rate bands are permissible only up to the date of separation. In order to determine who is the assessable spouse, one has to consider section 1017 and section 1019 TCA 1997. If the husband is the assessable spouse, then it is the wife who is taxed on her own income up to date of separation, with unused personal allowances and tax bands being transferred to the husband. The non-assessable spouse, *i.e.* the wife would be subject to tax in her own right from date of separation to the following April 5.

**Example**

Date of separation: July 5, 1999

Tax Bill for 1999/2000 for a couple earning income as follows:

|  |  | IR£ |
|---|---|---|
| Assessable spouse |  | 30,000 |
| Non-Assessable spouse – Up to July 5, 1999 |  | 1,250 |
| July 6, 1999 – April 5, 2000 |  | 3,750 |
|  |  | 5,000 |

(a) Assessable spouse (for full year)

|  |  |  |
|---|---|---|
| Total and Taxable Income |  | 30,000 |
| 18,000 at 24% | 3,360 |  |
| *12,750 at 46% (non-assessable spouse's unulised share) | 3,060 |  |
| 3,250 at 46% | 1,495 |  |
| 30,000 | 7,915 |  |
| Less: Personal Allowance |  |  |
| (£4,200 at 24%) | (1,008) |  |
| (*£2,950 at 24% – non-assessable spouse's unutilised share) | (708) |  |
| Tax Bill | 6,199 |  |
| After tax income (own only) | 23,801 |  |
| Net disposable income | 23,081 | (1) |

(1) £30,000 – £6,199 = £23,801

(b) Non-assessable spouse (Pre Separation)

| | |
|---|---:|
| Total and Taxable Income | 1,250 |
| 1,250  at 24% | 300 |
| Less:  Personal Allowance (£1,250 at 24%) | (300) |
| Tax Bill | Nil |

*Excess Personal Allowances of IR£2,950 granted at the standard rate plus IR£12,750 of the standard Tax Rate Band can be transferred to assessable spouse. (See (a) above)

(c) Non-assessable spouse (Post Separation)

| | |
|---|---:|
| Total and Taxable Income | 3,750 |
| 3,750  at 24% | 900 |
| Less:  Personal Allowance (£3,750 at 24%) | (900) |
| Tax Bill | Nil |

The married couple's tax bill in the tax year of separation is less than for a married couple living together, *i.e.* £6,199 and Nil = £6,199.

## Single Assessment

Each spouse continues as before to submit his/her own tax return and pay their own respective tax bills. There is no change to their tax status in the year of separation.

## 2.1.2  Subsequent Tax Years

If the separation extends beyond the tax year of separation, the married couple are treated as two single people for income tax purposes. They are assessable on their own income, required to submit their own tax returns and make timely tax payments.

## Example

Date of Separation: July 5, 1999

Tax Bill for 2000/01 for a separated couple earning income as follows:

(1999/2000 allowances and rates assumed to apply for 2000/01)

|  | | IR£ |
|---|---|---|
| High Income spouse | | 30,000 |
| Lower Income spouse | | 5,000 |

|  | Higher income spouse's Tax Bill IR£ |  | Lower income spouse's Tax Bill IR£ |  |
|---|---|---|---|---|
| Total and Taxable Income | 30,000 | | 5,000 | |
| 14,000 at 24% | 3,360 | 5,000 at 24% | 1,200 | |
| <u>16,000</u> at 46% | 7,360 | | | |
| <u>30,000</u> | 10,720 | | 1,200 | |
| Less: Personal Allowance (£4,200 at 24%) | (1,008) | (4,200 at 24%) | (1,008) | |
| | 9,712 | | 192 | 9,904 |
| Net disposable income | 20,288 | (2) | 4,808 | (2) |

(1)  £30,000 − £9,712 = £20,288
(2)  £5,000 − £192 = £4,808

The Income Tax Bill for 2000/2001 shows a substantial increase over the 1999/2000 Income Tax Bill for the tax year of separation or when they are living together:

| Living together (Para 1.1.2) | 7,924 |
|---|---|
| Tax year of separation  (Para 2.1.1) | 6,199 |
| Subsequent tax year (Para 2.1.2) | 9,904 |

Obviously, at this stage, the question of maintenance for a dependent spouse may need to be addressed. In many cases, arrangements regarding maintenance may be informal for a period of time.

There is no tax deduction available for voluntary maintenance payments as the statutory provisions only allow a deduction in computing total income for maintenance payments made under a legally binding document. Correspondingly, the receipt of voluntary maintenance payments is not taxable. In this context, voluntary maintenance can be defined as maintenance payments made without agreement of the payee spouse. The Revenue also consider verbal maintenance agreements as voluntary due to the anticipated difficulties in enforcing an oral agreement.

### 2.1.3 Interaction of Married Allowance and Voluntary Maintenance

If a husband is wholly or mainly maintaining his wife, he is entitled to the married allowance.[19] As a rule of thumb, the Revenue grant the married allowance provided maintenance payments to his wife exceed income earned in her own right.

Up to 1995/96 inclusive, if a wife wholly or mainly maintained her husband, she was not entitled to the married allowance.[20] For the tax year 1996/97 onwards, the married allowance is also given to a wife of the married couple not living together.

It is understood that the Revenue will only grant the married allowance to the wife provided her own maintenance payments to her husband exceed income earned in his own right.

Since 1993/94, the Revenue have, as a matter of practice, been granting the married allowance to a wife in the same circumstances as for a husband.

### Example

A couple living apart and one spouse is mainly maintained by the other spouse. Voluntary maintenance of IR£6,000 annually is paid. Income earned by each spouse in their own right.

---

[19] S. 461 (a) TCA 1997.
[20] First Schedule F.Act 1996.

|  | | | IR£ |
|---|---|---|---|
| High Income spouse | | | 30,000 |
| Lower Income spouse | | | 5,000 |

|  | Payer spouse's Tax Bill IR£ | | Payee spouse's Tax Bill IR£ |
|---|---|---|---|
| Income | 30,000 | | 5,000 |
| Maintenance receipt | | | n/a |
|  | 30,000 | | 5,000 |
| Less maintenance payment | n/a | | |
| 14,000 at 24% | 3,360 | 5,000 at 24% | 1,200 |
| 16,000 at 46% | 7,360 | | |
| 30,000 | 10,720 | | 1,200 |
| Less: Personal Allowance | | | |
| (8,400 at 24%) | (2,016) | (4,200 at 24%) | (1,008) |
|  | 8,704 | | 192 | 8,896 |
| After tax income | 21,296 | | 4,808 |
| Net disposable income | 15,296 | (1) | 10,808 |

(1)   £30,000 – (£6,000 + £8,704) = £15,296

(2)   £5,000 – (£192 + £6,000) = £10,808

Each spouse is taxed as a single person and the spouse paying the maintenance spouse obtains the married allowance.[21]

*Note 1*   If the annual voluntary maintenance figure is less than the income earned by the payee spouse, the revenue will not grant the married allowance to the payer spouse in practice.

*Note 2*   If the voluntary maintenance is split between the spouse and children, then the children's maintenance is excluded in determining the level of maintenance payments for the purpose of determining entitlement to married allowance.

---

[21] S. 461(a) TCA 1997.

### 2.1.4 Entitlement to Single Parent Allowance

When a married couple separate the children of the marriage may reside with either spouse for the full tax year. Alternatively, they may reside with both spouses at different times during the year. For example, the children may reside with the mother during the week and with the father at weekends or alternate weekends. In this situation, either or both spouses may be entitled to the single parent allowance.[22] For 1999/2000 this is IR£3,150 granted at the marginal rate and IR£1,050 granted at the standard rate, *i.e.* 24%.

For a parent to be entitled to this allowance, certain conditions must be fulfilled including:

- the child must be, during the tax year, under the age of eighteen years or, if over the age of eighteen years, attending full time education. Alternatively, the child must be permanently incapacitated by reason of mental or physical infirmity from maintaining himself and have become so permanently incapacitated before the age of 21 years or if over the age of 21 years was attending full time education or training at the time of his permanent incapacity[23];

- the child must be maintained at the parent's own expense for the whole or part of the tax year[24]; and

- the child must reside with the parent for the whole or part of the tax year. If the child is not a child of the parent then the parent must have custody of the child. Child includes a step child, a child whose parents have not married and an adopted child adopted under the Adoption Acts.[25]

If both spouses each maintain a child who resides with each parent for part of the tax year, it is possible for each parent to claim the full single parent allowance. The single parent allowance is not apportioned between the parents. Only one single parent allowance is given to a taxpayer irrespective of the number of children (even if there is only one child) that may qualify. Maintenance for this purpose can be either voluntary, by court order or by legal agreement.

---

[22] S. 462 and 462A TCA 1997.
[23] S. 462(1)(a)(i) TCA 1997 as amended by s. 55 FA 1999.
[24] S. 462(1)(a)(ii) TCA 1997.
[25] S. 462(2) TCA 1997.

## Example

A married couple living apart. Children reside with one spouse during the week and with other spouse at weekends. No maintenance in respect of the other spouse is payable by either spouse. Each spouse maintains the children when the children are residing with them. Income earned by each spouse in their own right.

|                     | IR£    |
|---------------------|--------|
| High Income spouse  | 30,000 |
| Lower Income spouse | 5,000  |

|                              | Payer spouse's Tax Bill IR£ |                    | Payee spouse's Tax Bill IR£ |       |
|------------------------------|-----------------------------|--------------------|-----------------------------|-------|
| Income                       | 30,000                      |                    | 5,000                       |       |
| Single parent allowance      | (3,150)                     |                    | (3,150)                     |       |
| Taxable income               | 26,850                      |                    | 1,850                       |       |
| 14,000 at 24%                | 3,360                       | 1,850 at 24%       | 444                         |       |
| 12,850 at 46%                | 5,911                       |                    | —                           |       |
| 26,850                       | 9,271                       |                    | 444                         |       |
| Less: Personal Allowance     |                             | (1,850 at 24%))    |                             |       |
| (4,200 at 24%)               | (1,008)                     | (1)                | (444)                       |       |
| Single Personal Allowance    |                             |                    |                             |       |
| (1,050 at 24%)               | (252)                       | (2)                | not utilised                |       |
|                              | 8,011                       |                    | nil                         | 8,011 |
| After tax income             | 21,989                      |                    | 5,000                       |       |
| Net disposable income        | 21,989                      | (3)                | 5,000                       |       |

(1)  Personal allowance limited to income taxable at the 24% rate.
(2)  No further income taxable at the 24% rate of tax
(3)  £30,000 − £8,011 = £21,989

Three exclusions apply. These include:

(a) If a spouse is entitled to the married allowance, he/she cannot claim the single parent allowance.[26]

(b) If a separated spouse starts a household with a new partner, he or she may not claim single parent allowance as the legislation precludes the relief being claimed where a man and woman are living together as husband and wife.[27]

(c) If a child has income in his or her own right, then the single parent allowance may be restricted. If the child's income exceeds £770 then the portion of the single parent allowances granted at the standard rate is reduced a pound for each pound by which the income exceeds £1,050. The amount of the single parent allowance, *i.e.* £3,150 for 1999/2000 is clawed back if the child's income exceeds IR£1,770. This is also done on a pound for pound basis. Scholarships, bursaries and other educational endowments are not taken into account as income for this purpose.[28]

### 2.1.5  Impact on Income Tax Reliefs – Mortgage Interest

When a couple separate, the tax reliefs available for mortgage interest relief may change.

If a couple separate and the higher income spouse continues to pay the mortgage repayments for the family home, then interest relief will be granted by the Revenue as if he/she were a single person.[29] This will have effect for the second tax year of separation onwards. The reason for this is that the married couples' increased interest relief provisions only apply where the couple are jointly or separately assessed, *i.e.* assessed under section 1017 TCA 1997.

It is also possible for a separated spouse to qualify for tax relief on interest payments both on his/her own residence and a separated spouse's residence. However, the single person's interest relief limit of IR£2,500 will still apply.

If a spouse claims tax relief for interest paid on a loan for his/her separated spouse's main residence, that interest will not be regarded

---

[26] S. 462(1)(b) TCA 1997.
[27] S. 462(2) TCA 1997.
[28] S. 462(5) TCA 1997.
[29] S. 244 TCA 1997.

as a maintenance payment. Therefore a spouse would not be entitled to married allowance unless further voluntary payments were made to wholly or mainly maintain his/her spouse and such payments exceed the income earned by the lower income spouse in his/her own right.

It should be noted that interest relief will not be available if the mortgage is in the name of say the lower income spouse and mortgage repayments are made by the higher income spouse who occupies the residence. This is due to the fact that the loan was not taken out by the spouse making the mortgage repayments.

## 2.2 PRSI AND HEALTH CONTRIBUTION LEVY (HCL)

When a couple separate the mere fact of separation does not give rise to any change in their respective PRSI and HCL liability.

Payment of voluntary maintenance does not give rise to a PRSI/HCL liability for the recipient spouse. The payer spouse cannot receive any refund of the HCL for income paid out as voluntary maintenance.

For the payer spouse PRSI refunds cannot be obtained for income paid out as voluntary maintenance.

However, see para 3.2 for PRSI/levies consequences where maintenance is paid under a court order.

## 3.1 DIVORCE

### 3.1.1 Maintenance

Perhaps the most common monetary aspect of any legal divorce is the maintenance aspect, *i.e* where one spouse has to pay moneys for the support of the other spouse and/or children. Essentially maintenance means being provided either directly or indirectly with basic living essentials such as accommodation, food, clothes etc. In order to obtain a tax deduction for maintenance payments, it is necessary for the maintenance provisions to comply with the requirements of section 1025 TCA 1997. These are:

### *Legally enforceable*

The maintenance arrangements must be legally enforceable and made or done in consideration or in consequence of a separation or divorce referred to in section 1015 TCA 1997. This separation may be factual or legal.

A maintenance arrangement is defined as "an order of court, deed of separation, rule of court, trust, covenant or any other act which gives rise to a legally enforceable obligation".

### Post June 7, 1983

The provision applies only to legal obligations arising after June 7, 1983. It can apply where a pre-1983 maintenance arrangement is replaced by another post June 7, 1983 arrangement or, in fact, where both parties governed by a pre-1983 maintenance arrangement jointly elect for the 1983 provisions to apply.

### Annual/Periodical

To qualify as maintenance payments for the purposes of section 1025 TCA 1997 the payments must be annual or periodic. Lump sum orders granted under section 13 (1) (c) and (2) Family Law (Divorce) Act 1996, do not qualify.

### Definition

To qualify as a maintenance payment under section 1025, a benefit must accrue to a child or other party of the marriage. Payments other than direct monetary payments to a child or other party of the marriage can qualify.

### No Deduction of Tax

Maintenance payments are paid without deduction of standard rate income tax (24% for 1999/2000). This is different from the pre – June 8, 1983 position.

### Spouse/Children

The legislative provisions distinguish between maintenance payments made to the children and maintenance payments made to a spouse.

If a payment is directed to be made for the sole use and benefit of a child of the payer; and the amount, or the method of calculating the amount, of such payment is specified in the maintenance arrangement, then:

- the payments must be paid gross (*i.e.* without deduction of tax);

- the payer is not entitled to a deduction in computing total income for the payments;

- the payments do not rank as income of the child and are not taxable.

The single parent allowance and/or incapacitated child allowance may be claimed as the payments, whether direct or indirect, are a contribution towards the child's maintenance. Examples of indirect child maintenance payments could include payment of the child's school fees, holidays, courses, activities, sports, etc.

A child includes:

(a)  a step child,[30]

(b)  a child adopted under the Adoption Acts 1952 to 1991, or

(c)  a child whose parents have not married.[31]

All other maintenance payments are deemed to relate to the spouse where payments under a maintenance arrangement are made directly or indirectly by one spouse for the benefit of the other spouse:

- the payment must be made gross;

- the payer is entitled to a tax deduction for the maintenance payments;

- the payee spouse is taxable on the maintenance receipts.

*Other Jurisdictions*

The provision is not confined to maintenance arrangements governed by Irish law only. It extends to maintenance arrangements made under any other jurisdiction also.

---

[30] S. 6 TCA 1997.
[31] S. 8 TCA 1997.

### 3.1.2 Tax Treatment – Single Persons

If a maintenance arrangement fulfils the conditions of section 1025 TCA 1997, the separated couple are treated for tax purposes as single persons, each liable to tax in their own right.

A tax deduction can be obtained by the paying spouse for any maintenance payments made to the other spouse. The tax deduction is applied in computing total income. However, no tax deduction is available for maintenance payments for the benefit of the children of the marriage as defined above.

The maintenance payments are taxable in the hands of the recipient spouse as Case IV income but he or she is entitled to a single persons allowance and single rate tax bands.

In addition, either spouse may be entitled to the single parent's allowance provided the child is of relevant age, resides with and is maintained by the claimant for the whole or part of the year of assessment. It is not necessary to have any formal wording in say for example a separation agreement as it is only necessary for the child to reside with and be maintained by the parent. The residence need only be part-time.

### Example

A couple separated, legally enforceable maintenance payable to lower income earning spouse of IR£6,000 annually – infant children reside with and to be supported by lower income earning spouse. Income earned by each spouse in own right. Single assessment under section 1025 TCA 1997 applies.

|                        |                                      |                                      | IR£    |
|------------------------|--------------------------------------|--------------------------------------|--------|
| High Income spouse     |                                      |                                      | 30,000 |
| Lower Income spouse    |                                      |                                      | 5,000  |

|                      | Payer spouse's Tax Bill IR£ | Payee spouse's Tax Bill IR£ |
|----------------------|-----------------------------|-----------------------------|
| Income               | 30,000                      | 5,000                       |
| Maintenance receipt  | —                           | 6,000                       |
|                      | 30,000                      | 11,000                      |

| | | | | |
|---|---|---|---|---|
| Maintenance payment | (6,000) | | — | |
| Total income | 24,000 | | 11,000 | |
| Less: Single parent allowance | — | | (3,150) | |
| Taxable income | 24,000 | | 7,850 | |
| 14,000 at 24% | 3,360 | 7,850 at 24% | 1,884 | |
| 10,000 at 46% | 4,600 | | — | |
| 24,000 | 7,960 | | 1,884 | |
| Less: Personal Allowance (£4,200 at 24%) | (1,008) | (4,200 at 24%) | (1,008) | |
| Single Personal Allowance (£1,050 at 24%) | — | (1,050 at 24%) | 252 | |
| | 6,952 | | 624 | 7,576 |
| After tax income | 23,048 | | 10,376 | |
| Net disposable income | 17,048 (3) | | 10,376 (2) | |

(1)  £30,000 – (£6,000 + £6,952) = £17,048
(2)  £11,000 – £624 = £10,376

### 3.1.3 Option for Joint Assessment

A married but separated couple can continue from a tax point of view as if they were not separated. To do this, there must be a maintenance arrangement as defined by section 1025 in existence, both parties must be resident in Ireland during the tax year and there must be a joint election in writing for the provision to apply. It applies to separated and divorced couples. For divorced couples each ex-spouse must fulfill a further condition, *i.e.* neither spouse must have remarried. [32]

At first sight, the provision is an election to joint assessment. The election for joint assessment is, in fact, a misnomer, as the legislation states that the separate assessment rules are to apply. Basically, this means that each spouse submits their own tax return, is entitled to his/her own personal allowances and tax rate bands but pays tax only on his/her own income. However, if either spouse has any unutilised personal allowances or tax rate bands, then these can be transferred

---

[32] S. 1026 TCA 1997.

to the other spouse. Since the decision to opt for section 1026 TCA 1997 is a joint one, the usual time limits for separate assessment do not apply. The election may be made at any time during the year. In this case the election cannot be "deemed" to apply and must be specifically requested.

The main tax consequences of such an election is that there is no deduction for any maintenance payments paid and no liability attaching to the maintenance received.[33]

Either party can withdraw from the election prior to the end of the tax year.[34]

## Example

Married couple separated. Legally enforceable maintenance arrangement entered into, with higher income spouse agreeing to pay maintenance of IR£6,000 annually. Income earned by each spouse in own right. Both spouses elect for joint assessment under section 1026 TCA 1997.

|  | | IR£ |
|---|---|---|
| Payer spouse | | 30,000 |
| Payee spouse | | 5,000 |

|  | Payer spouse's Tax Bill IR£ | | Payee spouse's Tax Bill IR£ |
|---|---|---|---|
| Income | 30,000 | | 5,000 |
| Maintenance receipt | — | | n/a |
|  | 30,000 | | 5,000 |
| Maintenance payment | n/a | | — |
| Total and taxable income | 30,000 | | 5,000 |
| 14,000 at 24% | 3,360 | 5,000 at 24% | 1,200 |
| *9,000 at 24% | 2,160 | | — |
| 7,000 at 46% | 3,320 | | — |
| 30,000 | 8,740 | | 1,200 |

---

[33] S. 1026(2) 1997.
[34] S. 1018(3) TCA 1997.

| | | | |
|---|---|---|---|
| Less: Personal Allowance | | | |
| (£4,200 at 24%) | (1,008) | (4,200 at 24%) | (1,008) |
| | 7,732 | 192 | 7,924 |
| After tax income | 22,268 | 4,808 | |
| Disposable income | 16,268 (1) | 10,808 (2) | |

(1)  £30,000 – (£7,732 + £6,000) = £16,268
(2)  £5,000 – £192 + £6,000 = £10,808

\* Balance of single rate tax bands in transferred to higher income spouse.

As a matter of practice, the Revenue, if it is clear that only one spouse will have an income for a particular year, will apply the joint assessment rules for the year instead of separate assessment. This would mean that the income earning spouse would be entitled to the married allowances and double rate tax bands. Only one return of income need be submitted.

### 3.1.4  Joint Assessment – Impact on Single Parent Allowance

Any decision to opt for joint assessment must take into account its impact on the entitlement to the single parent allowance.

If the joint assessment election is not made, each spouse is entitled to a single person's allowance.[35] In addition, any child who is both resident with and maintained by a spouse will entitle the spouse to the single parent's allowance. This need only be for part of the tax year. This could give the equivalent of four allowances to the two spouses, *i.e.* 2 single persons (IR£4,200 X 2) at the standard rate and two single parent's allowance (IR£3,150 X 2) granted at the marginal rate plus IR£1,050 x 2 granted at the standard rate. If a joint assessment election is made, only the married allowance, *i.e.* IR£8,400 granted at the standard rate, is available. The tax saving difference could amount to IR£3,402.

It can be seen that the net disposable income for the joint assessment couple, *i.e.* IR£27,076 (para 3.1.3) is less than for the couple who opt for single assessment, *i.e.* IR£27,424 (para 3.1.2). If the higher income spouse also claimed Single Parent Allowance, the net dis-

---

[35]  S. 462 TCA 1997.

posable income would be increased to IR£29,125. However, the lower income spouse, in the latter case, has an increased tax liability as the maintenance receipt is now taxable. This should be redressed by additional maintenance payments. It is necessary to prepare calculations on the after-tax income and net disposable income position to see the impact of any maintenance proposals and the joint/single assessment route.

### 3.1.5 Impact on Income Tax Reliefs – Mortgage

Any moneys paid under a legally enforceable maintenance arrangement can qualify for a tax deduction in computing total income for the payer provided there is no joint assessment election under section 1026 TCA 1997 (para 3.1.3).[36] These payments are then be taxable in the hands of the payee.

If the payee uses the moneys for expenditure which qualifies for tax relief, *e.g.* VHI premiums or interest paid on a mortgage on the principal private residence, then the *payee* will get a tax deduction subject to the normal income tax rules.

### Example

Married couple living apart. Legally enforceable maintenance arrangement entered into with higher income spouse agreeing to pay IR£6,000 maintenance annually to lower income spouse for his/her maintenance and two children. Lower income spouse to discharge mortgage repayments and VHI premiums from maintenance and own funds. Infant children reside with lower income spouse during the week and with other spouse on alternate weekends. Higher income spouse lives in rented accommodation. Income earned by each spouse in own right. Single assessment under section 1025 TCA 1997 applies.

|  | IR£ |
|---|---|
| Higher income spouse | 30,000 |
| Lower income spouse | 5,000 |
| VHI Premium (Plan B – 1 Adult and 2 children 1998 Rates and no group scheme discount) | 602 |
| Mortgage Interest payments (year 6 of mortgage) | 1,100 |

---

[36] S. 1025 TCA 1997.

Mortgage repayments
(£35,000 for 15 years at APR of 5.50%) say      4,800
Tax Relief on Mortgage Interest for non-first time
Mortgage holder      780
Rent payments      4,200

|  | Payer spouse's Tax Bill IR£ |  | Payee spouse's Tax Bill IR£ |  |
|---|---|---|---|---|
| Income | 30,000 |  | 5,000 |  |
| Maintenance receipt | — |  | 6,000 |  |
|  | 30,000 |  | 11,000 |  |
| Maintenance payment | (6,000) |  | — |  |
| Total income | 24,000 |  | 11,000 |  |
| Less: Single parent allowance | (3,150) |  | (3,150) |  |
| Taxable income | 20,850 |  | 7,850 |  |
| 14,000 at 24% | 3,360 | 7,850 at 24% | 1,884 |  |
| 6,850 at 46% | 3,151 |  | — |  |
| 20,850 | 6,511 |  | 1,884 |  |
| Less: Personal Allowance (4,200 at 24%) | (1,008) |  | (1,008) |  |
| Single Parent Allowance (1,050 at 24%) | (252) |  | (252) |  |
| Rent Allowance (max.) (500 at 24%) | (120) |  | — |  |
| VHI (602 at 24%) | — |  | (144) |  |
| Interest Relief (note) | — |  | (187) |  |
|  | 5,131 |  | 293 | 5,424 |
| After tax income | 24,869 |  | 10,707 |  |
| Net disposable income | 14,669 | (1) | 5,305 | (2) |

(1)  £30,000 − (£5,131 + £6,000 + £4,200) = £14,669
(2)  £5,000 + £6,000 − (£293 + £602 + £4,800) = £5,305

IR£

Note[37]

| | IR£ |
|---|---|
| Mortgage interest paid for 1999/2000 | 1,100 |
| Restricted at 80% | 880 |
| Less: First | (100) |
| Allowable interest relieved at 24% | 780 |

Alternatively, one spouse may discharge expenses directly such as VHI premiums, mortgage on principal private residence etc. It is possible for this spouse to obtain income tax relief for mortgage interest payments. If single assessment is opted for, the maximum interest relief available is for a single person only. If joint assessment applies, the interest relief is in fact doubled. For VHI payments, tax relief is available for VHI paid for the other spouse under the single or joint assessment routes, unless there is a divorce.

It is also possible to have the mortgage, *i.e.* capital and interest payments, treated as maintenance payments by the payer spouse. To qualify as a maintenance payment it must be for the benefit of the other spouse.

For example, a mortgage on the family home is in joint names and the couple make a maintenance arrangement whereby the higher income spouse discharges the mortgage repayments on the family home and the lower income spouse continues to live in it with the children. As the home is in joint names, the higher income spouse is still obliged to pay his/her half of the mortgage. The higher income spouses portion of the mortgage payment will qualify for interest relief but not as a payment for the other spouse's benefit and so not as maintenance.

The remainder may qualify for tax relief as maintenance. The lower income spouse would be taxable on these mortgage repayments made on his/ her behalf but will qualify for interest relief on the interest element.

Furthermore, the higher income spouse can choose between interest relief and maintenance in relation to his spouse's share of the mortgage repayments. However, it must be done on a consistent basis. In general, it is more tax effective for the payer spouse to have the other spouse's share of mortgage repayments treated as maintenance.

Similar comments would also apply to VHI premiums.

---

[37] S. 244 TCA 1997.

Where interest is treated as legally enforceable maintenance, it is not subject to the interest tax relief restrictions. The entire mortgage repayment, both interest and capital, is allowable without restriction as a maintenance deduction. It is possible, as part of the maintenance arrangement, to make two distinct sets of payments, of which one can be regarded as interest qualifying for tax relief as interest and the other as maintenance.

### 3.1.6 Variation of Type of Assessment

If the separated spouses agree, it is possible to change annually their decision between joint assessment and single assessment. Any decision to vary the previous year's treatment must, however, be notified to the Inspector of Taxes before the end of the tax year for which the new decision is to apply. A new decision for joint assessment must always be made by both spouses, but either spouse can revert back to assessment as single persons.

However, generally speaking, spouses do not tend to use this facility.

## 3.2 PRSI AND HEALTH CONTRIBUTION LEVY (HCL)

The question of PRSI and HCL on maintenance payments and receipts only arises if a married couple choose to be assessed as two single persons under section 1025 TCA 1997.

In the case of a spouse who is receiving maintenance payment from his/her spouse and is taxable as a single person in his/her own right, then he/she will have a liability for the tax year 1999/2000 to pay PRSI for the self employed at the rate of 5% up to total income of £25,400. PRSI is not payable if gross income including maintenance is less than £2,500.

PRSI for the self employed is not payable in respect of maintenance received if the recipient spouse pays PRSI as an employee. However, if the recipient spouse has trade or professional income as a self employed individual then PRSI will be payable on the maintenance receipt.[38]

In addition, Health Contributions at the rate of 2% are also due. This is not payable for 1999/2000 if his/her gross income including maintenance is £11,250 or less. These percentages amount to 7% and

---

[38] Para. 4 Pt III First Sched. S. W (Con) Act 1993.

can represent a fairly hefty outflow from the recipient's maintenance income.

In addition, as the maintenance paying spouse would, more than likely, have paid PRSI/HCL and levies on his/her own income, there is an element of double taxation.[39] This is a further factor which should be borne in mind when considering whether or not to opt for single or joint assessment. This element of double taxation has been rectified for HCL for 1995/96 onwards in the Social Welfare Act 1995. The maintenance paying spouse is entitled to a refund of HCL relating to income paid out as maintenance.

## Example

A couple separate and legally enforceable maintenance payable to lower income earning spouse of £6,000 annually. Infant children reside with and have to be supported by the lower income earning spouse. Income earned by each spouse:

|  |  | IR£ | IR£ |
|---|---|---|---|
| Higher income spouse |  |  | 30,000 |
| Lower income spouse |  |  | 5,000 |
| PRSI levies liability for 1999/2000 |  |  |  |
| <u>(a) Higher income spouse (Class C1)</u> |  |  | 30,000 |
| PRSI: weekly salary |  | 576.92 |  |
| Less: First £100 exemption |  | <u>(100.00)</u> |  |
|  |  | 476.92 |  |
| PRSI at 4.5% |  | 21.46 |  |
| This will be payable for 45 (44.03) weeks and amounts to |  |  | 944 |
| Levies: | Weekly salary | 576.92 |  |
|  | Payable at rate of 2% | 11.54 |  |
|  | Payable for 52 weeks | 600.00 |  |
|  | Less refund due on income paid out as maintenance (£6,000 at 2%) | <u>(120.00)</u> |  |
|  |  |  | 480 |
| **Total** |  |  | 1,425 |

*Note* This refund can only be obtained after the end of the tax year, *i.e.* April 5, 2000. The application is made to the Collector General.

---

[39] S. 25 Social Welfare Act 1995.

|  | IR£ | IR£ |
|---|---|---|
| (b) Lower income spouse (Class A0) |  | 5,000 |
| PRSI: weekly salary (note) | 96.15 |  |
| Less: First £100 exemption | (100.00) |  |
|  | Nil |  |
| PRSI at 4.5% | Nil |  |
| Total PRSI for 1999/2000 |  | 941 |

*Note* No PRSI is payable on maintenance as PRSI is paid as an employee. This includes all PRSI classes except Class S1. If income was self employed income, then the PRSI liability would be £498 (£5,000 + £6,000 − £1,040 @ 5%).

Levies

| Weekly salary | 96.15 |  |
|---|---|---|
| Weekly maintenance | 115.38 |  |
|  | 211.53 |  |
| Levies at 2% are not due as income is less than IR£217 weekly or IR£11,250 yearly | Nil |  |
| Total levies for 1999/2000 |  | Nil |
|  |  | Nil |

Where married couple opt to be taxed under section 1026 TCA 1997, then the maintenance payment and receipt is not recognised for income tax purposes and accordingly it is not recognised for PRSI or HCL purposes either.

## 4. FOREIGN DIVORCE

If a foreign divorce is granted which, as a matter of Irish law, is recognised here, then the following tax consequences should be noted.

### 4.1 INCOME TAX

Maintenance orders granted by a foreign court are recognised here for tax purposes.[40] Also from August 1, 1996 Irish courts can grant a relief order in relation to maintenance. Both types of maintenance orders will have the following tax consequences.

If both ex-spouses to the foreign divorce are resident in Ireland

---

[40] S. 1025 TCA 1997.

for tax purposes then the person making the maintenance payment will obtain a tax deduction in computing total income and the recipient will be taxed on maintenance received. The couple are taxed as two single people.

The difference between payments for the children and the ex-spouse apply as for a separated couple. [41]

If only the ex-spouse paying the maintenance is resident in Ireland for tax purposes, it does not preclude him/her obtaining a tax deduction for such payments. The extent to which the non-resident recipient ex-spouse is liable to Irish tax will depend on whether or not there is a Double Taxation Agreement between Ireland and the country of tax residence. If there is no Double Taxation Agreement then the maintenance income is subject to Irish tax at the standard rate (24% for 1999/00) upwards. There is no entitlement to personal allowances for a non-resident except in specified circumstances. There may be practical difficulties in taxing this income.[42]

If only the ex-spouse receiving the maintenance is tax resident here, then such income is taxable in Ireland and there is entitlement to full personal allowances and other reliefs. The non-resident paying ex-spouse is not entitled to a tax deduction save to the extent that he/she has Irish source income.

In general, foreign divorced couples, unlike separated couples, can only avail of single assessment.[43] There is one exception. Since August 1, 1996, it is now possible for such a couple to avail of the joint assessment option for a particular tax year under section 1026(3) TCA 1997 provided a number of conditions are complied with:

(a)  The foreign divorce is legally recognised in Ireland,

(b)  Both ex-spouses are tax resident in Ireland for the tax year and

(c)  Neither ex-spouse has remarried.

## 4.2  PRSI AND HEALTH CONTRIBUTION LEVY (HCL)

If both parties to the former marriage are tax resident in Ireland then the maintenance paying spouse will be liable to PRSI either as an employee or self employed person if under the age of 66 years. There

---

[41]  See para. 3.1.1.
[42]  S. 1032 TCA 1997.
[43]  S. 1026(3) TCA 1997.

is no relief for PRSI paid on income out of which maintenance payments are made. In the case of the recipient ex-spouse, no PRSI for the self employed is payable on maintenance payments if he/she pays PRSI as an employed contributor i.e. is an employee and does not have trade or professional income as a self employed individual. No PRSI is payable if his/her gross income including maintenance is less than £2,500.

The maintenance paying ex-spouse will receive a refund of levies referable to income paid out as maintenance. The recipient ex-spouse will only be liable to the 2% Health Contribution levy if his/her gross income including maintenance is £11,250 or more (1999/2000 limit).

If only the ex-spouse paying maintenance is resident here, then a refund of levies but not of PRSI can be obtained. The extent to which the ex-recipient spouse would be liable to pay levies on this income will depend on whether such income is taxable here in Ireland. This will follow the income tax position. If the income liable to Irish tax is less than £11,250 (1999/2000 limit), then the question of levies does not arise. On the question of PRSI, no PRSI is payable provided he/she is not resident or ordinarily resident in Ireland and is not in receipt of Schedule D Case I or II Irish source income.

Where only the recipient ex-spouse is resident in Ireland then such maintenance payments are subject to levies only if reckonable income including maintenance exceed £11,250 (1999/2000 limit). With regard to PRSI, he/she will only be liable to pay PRSI on such maintenance payments if he/she has trading or professional income.

## 4.3 Foreign divorce not recognised in Ireland

In general, if either party to a marriage which is recognised here go through divorce proceedings which are not legally recognised under common law or the Domicile and Recognition of Foreign Divorces Act 1986, then the couple are treated as a separated couple and the consequences as outlined in Para 3 will apply. This assumes that a maintenance order has been made in the divorce decree or a separate legal document has been drawn up regarding this issue.

### 4.3.1 Foreign divorce not recognised in Ireland followed by remarriage

If a couple obtain a foreign divorce which is not legally recognised in Ireland and one of the parties to the marriage remarries, then this marriage is not recognised in Ireland. Therefore, it is not possible for the newly married couple to obtain any tax benefits. This is subject to one exception. From an income tax point of view, it is current Revenue practice to recognise such a marriage if a foreign marriage certificate is produced. However, if the second marriage is subsequently challenged, the Revenue will follow the legal position.

## 5. ASSETS

## 5.1 CAPITAL GAINS TAX

### 5.1.1 Husband and wife living together

A marriage ceremony of itself does not give rise to any capital gains tax advantage. To obtain any capital gains tax benefits, a couple must be legally married and "living together".[44]

Under the capital gains tax rules a married couple are "living together" unless either:

> "(a) they are separated under an order of a Court of competent jurisdiction or by deed of separation, or
>
> (b) they are in fact separated in such circumstances that the separation is likely to be permanent ."[45]

Accordingly, it is assumed that a married couple is living together unless there is a definite separation, either by court order or as a matter of fact.

The advantages obtained by a married couple "living together" include:

–   Entitlement to be assessed jointly or separately,

–   Entitlement to dispose of assets to each other without being subject to CGT,

–   Each spouse is entitled to a £1,000 annual exemption, and

–   Capital losses available to one spouse can be used by the other spouse.

---

[44] S. 5(2) TCA 1997.
[45] S. 1015(2) TCA 1997.

## 5.1.2 Joint Assessment[46]

The tax due on gains arising to a married woman living with her husband in a tax year is normally assessed and charged on her husband. However the capital gains tax payable by the husband cannot exceed the capital gains tax bill if they were separately assessed. The Revenue can request that she submit a return. The wife can also be assessed to her share of capital gains tax under section 1022 TCA 1997 if her share of the capital gains tax remains unpaid. In addition, joint assessment can apply to gains arising in the year of marriage, *i.e.* from date of marriage to April 5.

As for income tax a wife can be the assessable spouse since April 6, 1994.[47]

## Separate Assessment[48]

An application for separate assessment can be made by either spouse giving notice in writing to the Inspector of Taxes within 3 months after the end of the relevant year of assessment. The application for a separate assessment is effective until it is withdrawn by the spouse who made the original application. This notice of withdrawal has no effect unless it is given within 3 months after the end of the tax year for which it is to take effect. Where such an election is made by either spouse, both are separately assessed for capital gains tax.

## 5.1.3 Disposal of Assets Between Spouses[49]

If spouses are living together, disposals from one to the other are treated as being made at such a price as will give no gain or loss to the spouse making the disposal.

The above exemption supersedes the imposed "arms length" provisions normally applied between connected persons.[50] The normal rule for acquisitions/disposals between connected persons is that the assets are deemed to be acquired/disposed of at market value.

However, this exemption does not apply if the assets disposed of

---

[46] S. 1028(1) TCA 1997.
[47] S. 931 TCA 1997.
[48] S. 1028(2) TCA 1997.
[49] S. 1028(5) and (6) TCA 1997.
[50] Ss. 10 and 549 TCA 1997.

are trading stock of the spouse making the disposal, or if the assets form part of the trading stock of the spouse acquiring them.

On a subsequent disposal, the spouse acquiring the asset is treated as if that spouse had acquired the asset at the same date and cost as the disposing spouse had originally acquired it.

### 5.1.4 Annual Exemption[51]

Each tax payer is entitled to realise an annual real gain after inflation of £1,000 before being subject to CGT on any excess at the rate of 20%, or in the case of certain assets 40%.[52] The annual exemption is similar to an income tax personal allowance in that if it is not used in one tax year, it cannot be carried forward.

In the case of a husband and wife where both are chargeable to capital gains tax in a tax year (or would be so chargeable but for the annual exemption) and the gains of one spouse are less than £1,000, the unutilised portion of the annual exemption can be used by the other spouse, in addition to that individuals own annual exemption. This applied up to April 5, 1998.

Since April 6, 1998, spouses cannot transfer their utilised annual exemption to each other.[53]

### 5.1.5 Losses[54]

Losses realised by one spouse in a tax year and not absorbed by his/her gains can be set against the gains of the other spouse arising in that year. This applies not only to losses in the current year, but also to losses coming forward from previous years.

This provision does not apply if either spouse gives notice to that effect within three months after the tax year to the Inspector of Taxes. Where such a notice is given, the losses are carried forward against subsequent gains of the spouse to whom the losses accrued.

### 5.2 CAPITAL ACQUISITIONS TAX (CAT)

All gifts and inheritances given by one spouse to another are exempt from capital acquisitions tax.

---

[51] S. 601 TCA 1997.
[52] Ss. 28 and 601, TCA 1997; S. 65 F. Act 1998.
[53] S. 75 F. Act 1998.
[54] S. 1028(3) TCA 1997.

Inheritances have only been exempt since January 30, 1985.[55] If at the date of the inheritance the recipient is the spouse of the donor, then the inheritance is exempt from inheritance tax and does not have to be taken into account in calculating CAT on later gifts or inheritances from any spouse.

This exemption was subsequently extended to gifts with effect from 31 January 1990 where a gift is taken by an individual who at the date of the gift is the spouse of the donor.[56] Again, the gift is not taken into account in computing tax on later gifts or inheritances.

In the period from January 30, 1985 to January 30, 1990, the CAT exemption applied only to inheritances and did not extend to gifts unless the donor died within 2 years of the gift and the date of the gift was on or after January 30, 1985.

## 5.3 STAMP DUTY

A married couple have always been entitled to reliefs from the normal rates of stamp duty for any property other than stocks and shares. Up to July 17, 1982, the rate of stamp duty on the transfers of assets between spouses was 1%. Thereafter, the duty payable was restricted to 50% of the duty that would otherwise be payable.[57]

The first full relief was only introduced in section 14 of the Family Home Protection Act 1976. This section relieved fully from stamp duty the charge arising where the family home (as defined) was transferred into the joint names of the two spouses where the home immediately prior to such a transaction was owned by either spouse or both spouses otherwise than as joint tenants.

This relief was further extended in the Finance Act 1990 to include the transfer of all assets.[58] The exemption now includes a direct transfer from one spouse to another or a transfer from one spouse into the joint names of both spouses. No adjudication is required.

The stamp duty exemption does not apply if the instrument transferring the property includes a transfer to a person other than the spouse.

For example, if assets are transferred by way of trust to a spouse for life and on the death of the spouse to the children in equal shares,

---

[55] S. 59 F. Act 1985.
[56] S. 127 F. Act 1990.
[57] Sched. 4 F.Act 82.
[58] S. 114 F. Act 1990 as amended by s. 212 F. Act 1992.

then the stamp duty exemption will not apply. However, if the property is transferred into a spouse's name first and that spouse creates a trust in favour of himself/herself for life and on his/her death to the children in equal shares, then the value of the property referable to the full interest followed by the creation of the life interest taken by the spouse is exempt from stamp duty. The value of the life interest for stamp duty purposes is calculated by reference to the Life Interest Tables set out in Schedule 2 to the Capital Acquisitions Tax Act 1976. The remainder interest being transferred to the children, *i.e.* market value less life interest attributable to spouse would attract a stamp duty rate equal to 50% of the *ad valorem* rate.

## 5.4 PROBATE TAX[59]

When probate tax was first introduced, the transfer of assets, other than the dwelling house (as defined), by will or intestacy to a surviving spouse was not exempt from probate tax.[60] However, this was rectified retrospectively in the Finance Act 1994.

If a spouse receives assets absolutely, no probate tax is payable.[61] However, if assets are left to a spouse, *e.g.* by way of a trust for life then the payment of Probate Tax is deferred until the spouse, *i.e.* life tenant, dies.

If the surviving spouse gives up his/her limited interest for a cash sum, then no probate tax is due on part of the trust assets.[62] This is calculated by reference to the proportion which the cash received bears to the value of the trust assets at the surrender date.

It should also be noted that where the same property is held by one or more persons including the spouse, then only the probate tax relating to the share owned by the spouse is reduced to nil.[63]

---

[59] Chap. 1 Pt VI, F. Act 1993.
[60] S. 109(1) F. Act 1993.
[61] S. 115A(1)(b) F.Act 1993.
[62] S. 115A(1)(c) F. Act 1993.
[63] S. 115A(1)(a) F.Act 1993.

## 6. TRANSFER OF ASSETS

Both formal and informal separations are recognised for capital gains tax purposes. See comments in paragraph 2.1 regarding a definition of "living apart".

### 6.1 CAPITAL GAINS TAX (CGT)

From a capital gains tax point of view it is important to try to be definitive with regard to the date on when the separation is likely to be permanent. This is important for a number of reasons.

#### 6.1.1 Joint/Separate Assessment

While a married couple are living together, the tax due on gains arising to a married woman living with her husband in a tax year are assessed and charged on her husband[64] unless the married couple have opted for the wife to be the assessable spouse. This will only apply up to the date that the separation is likely to be permanent. From that date, the non-assessable spouse, *i.e.* normally a wife, is assessed in her own name in relation to any gains arising after the date of likely permanent separation.

In the case of separate assessment, there is no change, *i.e.* each spouse is separately assessed in respect of their respective gains. If the claim for separate assessment is withdrawn for a particular tax year prior to July 6, after the end of the tax year, then the joint assessment rules, as outlined above, will apply for the tax year of separation.

#### 6.1.2 Transfer of Assets

From the date that the separation is likely to be permanent, any transfer of assets between spouses is not exempt from CGT. This is different to income tax as the exemption only applies to the tax year or part of a tax year that the married couple are living together.

---

[64] S. 1028 (1) TCA 1997.

**Voluntary transfer of assets**

Although it is unusual for the transfer of assets to occur outside any legal arrangement relating to the separation, any such transfer could give rise to a capital gains tax liability unless an exemption or relief can be obtained. As the couple are still married, they are connected persons and market value will apply to the asset being transferred.[65] Therefore the person acquiring the asset, and the person making the disposal are treated as parties to a transaction otherwise than by way of a bargain made at arms length.

Section 547 TCA 1997 then provides that a person's disposal of an asset is deemed to be for a consideration equal to the market value of the asset where he disposes of an asset otherwise than by way of a bargain made at arms length. Similarly a person's acquisition of such an asset is deemed to be for a consideration equal to its market value.

**Example 1**

Married couple are separated in circumstances likely to be permanent since July 6, 1990. One of the assets owned by the couple is the former marital house which the lower income spouse has occupied with the children since July 6, 1990. The family home was purchased in their joint names on January 6, 1980. It is now agreed that the higher income spouse will transfer voluntarily his/her share in the family home. The current value of the house is £200,000. The house cost £40,000 including expenses on 6 January 1980. The transfer date is July 6, 1999.

A capital gains liability for the transferring spouse arises as follows:

---

[65] Ss. . 10 and 549 TCA 1997.

|                                   | IR£      | IR£       |
|-----------------------------------|----------|-----------|
| Market value (50% share)          |          | 100,000   |
| Less:   Cost of 50% share         | 20,000   |           |
| Index factor at 3.139             |          |           |
| Indexed cost                      |          | (62,780)  |
| Chargeable gain                   |          | 37,220    |

Period of ownership 19 years + 6 months
Principal private residence exemption applies
to period of actual occupation plus last 12 months
i.e. 11 years + 6 months (S604 TCA 1997)

Exempt gain: $37,220 \times \dfrac{11.5}{19.5}$

|                                   |          |           |
|-----------------------------------|----------|-----------|
|                                   |          | (21,950)  |
| Net chargeable gain               |          | 15,270    |
| Less: annual exemption            |          | (1,000)   |
| Taxable gain                      |          | 14,270    |
| Capital gains tax @ 20% payable on 1 November 1999 |  | 2,854     |

## Example 2

As part of the voluntary arrangement, the lower income spouse agrees
to transfer to the higher income spouse 1,000 shares in an investment
company owned equally by the married couple. The company was
set up in May 1986 and the 1,000 £1 ordinary shares were issued at
par. The shares are now valued at £11 each. A CGT computation
must be prepared for the lower income spouse.

|                                   | IR£      | IR£       |
|-----------------------------------|----------|-----------|
| Market value at 6 July 1999       |          | 11,000    |
| Less:   Cost in May 1986          | 1,000    |           |
| Index factor at 1.373             |          |           |
| Indexed cost                      |          | (1,373)   |
| Chargeable gain                   |          | 9,627     |
| Less:   Annual exemption          |          | (1,000)   |
| Taxable gain                      |          | 8,627     |
| Capital gains tax @ 20% payable on 1 November 1999 |  | 1,725     |

### 6.1.3 Annual Exemption

Up to April 5, 1998 inclusive, a spouse could transfer his/her unused annual exemption to his/her spouse. Unless a couple separated in circumstances likely to be permanent on April 6, the benefit of section 1028(4) TCA 1997 could be availed of, *i.e.* a spouse's unutilised annual exemption could be used by the other spouse. If one spouse had a gain less than IR£1,000, the excess would, under section 1028(4) TCA 1997, be transferred to the other spouse. Unlike income tax, the total exemption available for the tax year of separation could not exceed IR£2,000. If one spouse had no gains, as a matter of practice, the other spouse could obtain the full IR£2,000 annual exemption even if a gain arose after the date of likely permanent separation. To this extent, the annual exemption was treated like a personal allowance. Once available on April 6, it could not be withdrawn due to a change of circumstances during the tax year.

Since April 6, 1998, a spouse's annual exemption is not transferable to the other spouse. Therefore, the tax year of separation has no impact on the allocation of the annual exemption.

### 6.1.4 Losses

To the extent that losses crystallised by a spouse have not been used by his/her spouse, then any unused remaining losses as at the date of likely permanent separation can only be used by the spouse in whose favour they arose. That spouse can utilise those remaining losses against any gains arising after the date of likely permanent separation.

### 6.2 CAPITAL ACQUISITIONS TAX

Separation does not change the gift/inheritance exemption available for spouses whose marriage at the date of the gift/inheritance is recognised as valid in Ireland.

### Voluntary Transfer of Assets

The transfer of the marital home and shares from one spouse to the other in paragraph 6.1.2 does not give rise to a CAT problem.

### 6.3 STAMP DUTY

As for paragraph 6.2 (paragraph 1.3).

## 6.4 PROBATE TAX

As for 6.2 (paragraph 1.4).


# 7. DIVORCE

The transfer of one or more assets will arise in divorce cases. The capital gains tax exemption for transfer of assets between spouses living together has been extended to divorce.[66]

### 7.1.1 Capital Gains Tax – Family Home

The most common asset likely to be transferred is the "family home". For example, it may be ordered that the "family home" should be transferred into the name of one spouse. If so, then no capital gains tax liability will arise.

Alternatively, the "principal private residence" or "family home" could be dealt with in a number of other ways including:

> House placed into joint names of spouses on a trust for sale postponed until the youngest of the children is fully educated.

In the United Kingdom, this type of arrangement is known as a *Mesher Order*. It is based on a UK case called *Mesher v. Mesher and Hall.*[67] In that case, the family home was jointly owned and there was a young child aged nine. It was ordered that the family home should be held in trust for the spouses in equal shares, but that the house should not be sold so long as the youngest child was under 17, or until further order. In the meantime, the wife had the right to live in the house rent free provided she discharged all outgoings.

For capital gains tax, the key issue is whether a *Mesher Order* creates a settlement. The UK Revenue take the view that a *Mesher Order* creates a settlement on the basis that the initial transfer of the "family home" to the spouses as trustees on trust for sale is a disposal of their interest in the home, irrespective of the fact that they may also be trustees and beneficiaries.[68] The transfer is deemed to take place at the market value. However, because of the "principal private

---

[66] S. 1031 TCA 1997.
[67] [1981] All E.R. 126.
[68] CGT Manual, Vol. 6, para 65367.

residence" exemption, there will be no CGT liability for the spouse who has remained in the "family home". There will be a liability for the non occupying spouse if the *Mesher Order* is created more than one year after he/she permanently left the "family home".

When the *Mesher Order* terminates on the child having reached the age specified in the order, the husband and wife in their capacity as trustees of the settlement are deemed to have disposed of the house and immediately reacquired it as bare trustees for themselves. However, for the duration of the *Mesher Order* a trust beneficiary, the wife, was entitled to occupy the house as her main residence under the terms of the order. Consequently, under section 604(10) TCA 1997, the trustees should be entitled to claim "principal private residence" exemption in respect of the gain arising during the period of the trust. However, a taxable gain may arise if there is a delay in selling the house after termination of the *Mesher Order* when the child reaches the specified age. The spouse who has departed will have a chargeable gain of the difference, after indexation between that spouse's share of the sale proceeds and the market value of the house when the *Mesher Order* was terminated. Any such gain is likely to be small.

On the other hand, if the order does not create a settlement, a capital gains tax liability will not arise on the initial transfer of the house into joint ownership or as tenants in common even if the sole owner of the property prior to the transfer has not occupied it as his/her "principal private residence" for a period of time.

A variant of the order could require a husband who owned the house to put it into joint names of himself and his wife, and that they should thereafter own it in equal (or other) shares, with the sale being postponed. A further variant would be where the order expressly excluded the husband, from occupation of the "family home". In such cases it is the writers view that a settlement is not created. It is also the writers view that the wording in the *Mesher Order* can affect the tax consequences.

On the eventual sale of the property the non-occupying spouse will have a CGT liability because he/she may not have occupied the house as his/her "principal private residence" for several years.

*Mesher Orders* are not common in Ireland.

> House transferred to one spouse, giving the other a charge on the property. The charge cannot be realised until a specific event. The charge may be of a fixed amount (i.e. IR£30,000) or for a share (i.e.50%).

From a tax point of view, the initial transfer will not give rise to a capital gains tax charge.

On sale of the house, no capital gains tax liability should arise if the house has been occupied as the principal private residence of the owner.

A problem may arise for the non-occupying spouse when the agreed portion of the sale proceeds are paid over. In the view of the writer, this CGT problem only arises if there is a variable deferred charge, *e.g.* charge represents a share in the property. In essence, a variable deferred charge is a debt owed to the non occupying spouse. A debt is an asset under section 532(1) TCA 1997. The realisation of the deferred charge by the person in whose favour it has been granted will constitute a disposal. However, section 541 TCA 1997 provides that no chargeable gain shall accrue to the original creditor, or his personal representatives, on the disposal of a debt, other than a debt on a security. It would appear that the variable deferred charge would not be a "debt on a security" as considered by the House of Lords in *Aberdeen Construction Limited v. IRC*,[69] *WT Ramsey Ltd v. IRC*[70] and *Taylor Clarke International Ltd v. Lewis.*[71] The House of Lords, while finding the meaning of the phrase obscure, held that it was not synonymous with a secured debt. Rather, it envisaged a debt which has characteristics attached to it which would enable it to be marketed.[72]

However, while it can be accepted that the variable deferred charge is not a "debt on a security", one needs to consider the meaning of "debt" in section 541 TCA 1997 as outlined in the House of Lords decision *Marren v. Ingles.*[73] The issue considered by this case has not come before an Irish Court to date. In *Marren v. Ingles*, the taxpayer sold shares in the company for a fixed sum per share plus the right, in circumstances which might never occur, to receive a percentage of the value of the shares when they were resold by the purchaser. The taxpayer received additional payments when the shares were resold. The UK Revenue sought to charge capital gains tax on the additional monies received by the taxpayer. The House of Lords held that an asset was not a debt for the purposes of section 251(1)

---

[69] [1978] S. T.C. 127.
[70] [1981] S. T.C. 174.
[71] [1997] S. T.C. 499.
[72] *per* Lord Wilberforce in *Ramsey* at 184.
[73] [1980] S. T.C. 500.

TCGA 1992 (Irish equivalent to section 541(1) TCA 1997) where it was a *possible* liability to pay an *unidentifiable* sum at an *unascertainable* date. Unlike the debt considered in *Marren v. Ingles*, a deferred charge on the "family home" is certain to mature at some future date, but both the timing and the amount receivable are uncertain. It seems possible, in the light of other dicta in the *Marren v. Ingles* case, that Irish courts could regard these two factors as sufficient to preclude the deferred charge from taking advantage of the exemption for debts in section 541 TCA 1997. Consequently, the non-occupying spouse could have a chargeable gain of the amount he/she receives on the realisation of the charge, less the indexed market value of the charge at its date of acquisition. However, the market value at its date of acquisition needs to be determined. It would appear that the relevant question is: at date of creation of the charge, what could this right to receive a stated percentage of the eventual sale proceeds of the house be worth on the open market?

To summarise, in the case of a deferred variable charge, there is a disposal of the house to the other spouse which qualifies for the exemption under section 1030 TCA 1997. At the same time, the transferor spouse is acquiring a new asset, *i.e.* right to receive deferred consideration. This right has to be valued at date of acquisition. It is the writer's view that the value would equal the market value of the transferor spouse's interest in the house at the date of the transfer to the other spouse.

If the deferred charge is fixed i.e. represented by a sum of money in favour of the non occupying spouse, this deferred charge should constitute a debt within section 541 TCA 1997. This assumes that he/she had disposed of his/her whole ownership of the house in return for the deferred charge. Consequently, any gain on the disposal of the house should be realised at the time of transfer to the occupying spouse, and there will be no capital gains tax charge when the deferred charge is ultimately realised. This interpretation is assisted by section 563(1) TCA 1997 which enacts that the gain on the disposal of an asset is to be computed initially without regard to any postponement of the right to receive the consideration. In *Marson v. Marriage*[74] it was held that the UK equivalent of this subsection, *i.e.* section 48 TCGA 1992 presupposed a future consideration which was ascertainable in amount, and therefore had no application to a

---

[74] [1980] S. T.C. 177.

deferred consideration of uncertain amount. Conversely, it would appear that section 563(1) TCA 1997 should apply to a fixed consideration.

House placed in trust to spouse for life and thereafter to children.

In this situation, a settlement is being created. There would be a disposal from one spouse to the trustees and a capital gains tax charge may arise.[75]

On the death of the life tenant no capital gains tax charge arises on the transfer of the "family home" by the trustees to the children.

Sole occupancy given to one spouse for so long as the youngest child is under 18 years and thereafter to be sold with sale proceeds divided on an agreed basis.

If the "family home" is in the sole name of the non-occupying ex-spouse then, on the sale of the family home, a capital gains tax problem will arise for him/her as the house would not have been occupied as his/her "principal private residence". Accordingly, a portion of the gain arising on the disposal of the property would be subject to capital gains tax. The taxable portion of the gain would be computed by reference to the period of non-occupation of the residence (excluding the last twelve months of ownership) over the total period of ownership.

Similarly, even in the case of joint ownership, the non-occupying spouse could have a capital gains tax liability on the disposal of his/her half share in that property. On the other hand, it is unlikely that the occupying spouse would have a capital gains tax liability as the house had been occupied by him/her as his/her principal private residence throughout the period of ownership.

For example, the Court may order that 50% of the net proceeds of sale are to be given to the occupying spouse in the case of a property owned by the non-occupying spouse. If the non-occupying spouse realises a gain on the disposal of the property and has to pay capital gains tax on part of the gain, then the 50% share of the net sale proceeds payable to the occupying spouse is not reduced to take account of this fact.

---

[75] Ss. 575 and 577 TCA 1997.

### 7.1.2  Capital Gains Tax and Other Taxes – Other Assets

The transfer of other assets by order of the Court may also arise. If so, then both capital gains tax and other taxes may need to be considered.

For example, a court order may be made stating that trading assets owned jointly by the spouse as partners should be transferred to one spouse. In this situation, no capital gains tax liability will arise. However, upon transfer of the partnership assets to one spouse, there is a cessation of the partnership trade for income tax purposes. This means that the cessation of trade rules will come into play for both spouses. In addition, a balancing allowance/charge may arise on the transfer of assets which qualified for capital allowances. In some circumstances, it is possible to avoid the balancing allowance/charges by, for example, a joint election claim under section 289 (5) TCA 1997 for plant and machinery. The spouse acquiring the partnership assets will be subject to the commencement of trade rule for income tax. If the partnership carried on a farming trade and income averaging was claimed, the cessation of the partnership trade will give rise to a review of the income averaged for the two years prior to the last year of averaging. In addition, the spouse acquiring the partnership assets cannot claim income averaging until the fourth tax year of trading in his/her own name. These are some of the other tax issues which need to be considered if there is a transfer of business assets.

### 7.1.3  Financial Compensation Orders

Under section 16 FL (D) A 1996, the court can make a financial compensation order requiring either or both spouses to:

(i)   Effect a life insurance policy for the benefit of a spouse or dependent member of the family,

(ii)  Assign a life insurance policy to their spouse or dependent member of the family, or

(iii) To make or continue life insurance policy premium payments as required under the policy.

There are no tax implications arising from the making of such orders as outlined in (i) and (iii) above either on foot of payment of the life insurance premiums or payment of the life insurance policy proceeds. However, in the latter case, if the life insurance policy proceeds are paid to a dependent member of the family, then capital acquisitions tax may be an issue.

With regard to (i) above, the assignment of a life insurance policy to a spouse or dependent member of the family will not give rise to any capital gains tax or capital acquisitions tax problems. However, the payment of the life insurance policy proceeds is a disposal by the spouse or dependent member of the family for capital gains tax purposes. Under section 593 TCA 1997, if the person making the disposal is not the original beneficial owner and he/she acquired the rights or interests for a consideration in money or moneys worth, then capital gains tax may be an issue. It may be necessary to consider this in particular situations. For example, if the assignment of the life insurance policy arises on foot of a court order then no capital gains tax charge will arise under section 593 TCA 1997 as there has been no acquisition for a consideration in money or moneys worth. However, if the assignment results under the terms of a settlement, then section 593 TCA 1997 may need to be considered. The payment of the life insurance policy proceeds to a dependent member of the family will have capital acquisitions tax implications.

### 7.1.4 Secured Periodical Payments Orders

Under section 13(1)(b) FLDA 1996, the courts have power to award secured maintenance for a spouse and/or dependent member of the family. A secured periodical payments order could be defined as a maintenance order the payment of which is secured against a non income producing asset such as land.

It could also, as in the UK, mean that one spouse is required to transfer income producing assets, such as shares, to trustees with the trust income being used to pay maintenance to the other spouse. If the obligation to pay maintenance ceases, say on the death of a spouse, the trust ends and the assets revert to the settlor spouse. The latter type of secured periodical payments orders could cause capital gains tax difficulties. A transfer of income producing assets into a trust appears to constitute the creation of a settlement which, while the trust continues, the transferor cannot claim to be absolutely entitled as against the trustees. The transfer of the assets into a trust therefore constitutes a chargeable disposal for capital gains tax purposes, notwithstanding the fact that the transferor may retain an interest in the trust capital. The transferor spouse and trustees are connected persons and the transfer is therefore deemed to be made for a consideration equal to the market value of the assets at the date of transfer. The exemption available in section 1030 TCA 1997 cannot be availed of as the disposal is not to the other spouse.

If and when the obligation to pay maintenance ceases, the transferor spouse becomes absolutely entitled as against the trustees to a return of the assets. The trustees will therefore be deemed to have disposed of and reacquired the assets at their market value with a consequent potential chargeable gain, unless the reason for the reversion is the death of the spouse entitled to the maintenance. In the latter case, the transferor spouse will normally reacquire the assets at market value at the date of death.[76] At present secured periodical payments orders are not common. Attachment of earnings orders are used instead.

## 7.2 CAPITAL ACQUISITIONS TAX (CAT)[77]

As for capital gains tax, property transfers between former spouses following a court order governing a divorce is exempt for capital acquisitions tax. A legal separation or judicial separation does not have an impact on the capital acquisition tax exemptions for spouses.[78]

## 7.3 STAMP DUTY[79]

As for capital acquisitions tax.[80]

## 7.4 PROBATE TAX

If an ex-spouse dies, the surviving ex-spouse provided he/she has not remarried can apply for provision out of the estate of the deceased ex-spouse.[81]

No probate tax is payable on assets transferred to an ex-spouse following an order under section 18 FL (D) A 1996.[82]

Otherwise as for capital acquisitions tax.[83]

---

[76] S. 577 TCA 1997.
[77] S. 142 F. Act 1997.
[78] Para 6.2.
[79] S. 127 F. Act 1997.
[80] See para 7.2.
[81] S. 18 FL (D) A 1996.
[82] S. 143 F. Act 1997.
[83] Para 7.2.

## 8. FOREIGN DIVORCE RECOGNISED IN IRELAND

If a foreign divorce is granted which, as a matter of Irish law, is recognised here the tax consequences following the transfer of assets on foot of the foreign divorce decree are as follows:

### 8.1 Capital Gains Tax

Prior to August 1, 1996, the transfer of assets between spouses once they ceased living together did not qualify for the exemption under section 1028 TCA 1997. Any transfer of assets between ex-spouses following the divorce decree will be liable to capital gains tax if the ex-spouse transferring the asset(s) is resident or ordinarily resident in Ireland. In the case of a non-resident ex-spouse transferring assets, the transfer of certain assets, *e.g.* Irish land and buildings will be liable to capital gains tax.

Where a foreign divorce is granted which is recognised here and a relief order is granted then the transfer of assets arising from such a relief order qualifies for an exemption similar to the section 1028 (5) TCA relief. This is provided for in section 1030 (2) TCA 1997. This capital gains tax exemption does not apply to trading stock disposed of or acquired by either spouse.

### 8.2 Capital Acquisitions Tax (CAT)

Once a couple obtain a foreign divorce which is recognised here then the capital acquisitions tax exemption for gifts or inheritances passing between ex-spouses ceases. Accordingly, any transfer of assets between the spouses following the divorce decree could attract a capital acquisitions tax liability if the transferor ex-spouse is domiciled in Ireland or if the asset transferred is situated in Ireland.

If a relief order is obtained, assets can be transferred from one ex-spouse to the other without any capital acquisitions tax consequences. If a relief order is obtained from an Irish court for the transfer of assets from the estate of a former deceased spouse, then the capital acquisitions tax exemption will apply to such a transfer.[84]

---

[84] S. 142 F.Act 1997.

## 8.3 Stamp Duty

Any asset transferred following the divorce decree will attract the
normal stamp duty exemption similar to the capital acquisitions tax
exemption and is available if assets are transferred on foot of a relief
order.[85]

## 8.4 Probate Tax

On the death of a spouse, the passing of assets whether by absolute or
limited interest to the other spouse results in an abatement/postpone-
ment of the tax. Obviously, if couples are divorced, no such relief is
available. However, probate tax is abated to nil in the case of an absolute interest and postponed in the case of a limited interest in respect of assets given to a former spouse as a result of a relief order.[86]

## 8.5 Foreign Divorce not recognised in Ireland

In general, if either party to a marriage which is recognised here go
through divorce proceedings which are not legally recognised, then
the couple are treated as a separated couple and the consequences as
outlined in paragraph 6 will apply on the transfer of assets. For capital gains tax purposes a deed of separation would have to be in place
if the exemption under section 1030 TCA 1997 is being claimed. For
the other capital taxes, this is not necessary as there is no change in
their legal status as a married couple.

### 8.5.1 Foreign divorce not recognised in Ireland followed by remarriage

If a couple obtain a foreign divorce which is not legally recognised in
Ireland and one of the parties to the marriage remarries, then this
marriage is not recognised in Ireland. Therefore, it is not possible for
the newly married couple to obtain any tax benefits. This is subject to
one exception. From a capital gains tax point of view, it is current
revenue practice to recognise such a marriage if a foreign marriage
certificate is produced. This recognition does not apply to capital

---

[85] S. 127 F. Act 1997.
[86] S. 143 F. Act 1997.

acquisitions tax, stamp duty or probate tax. However, if the second marriage is subsequently challenged, the revenue will follow the legal position.

# Chapter 5

# Pensions and Divorce

## John D. McCarthy*

### 1. INTRODUCTION

This chapter is based upon practical experience to date and is intended to highlight some of the key issues affecting the resolution of pension and life insurance issues within Family Law Act situations. A number of aspects are identified in this chapter which I consider to require further discussion within the legal profession. I also refer to what I consider to be weaknesses in the legislation which require amendment.

### 2. THE SCOPE OF FAMILY LAW ACT ORDERS

The orders which may be made by family law courts are defined in legislation and need not be described in detail in a book of this nature. Nevertheless, there have been some common misunderstandings and problems regarding the particular types of orders. These can be summarised within the context of the following.

### (a) Retirement Benefits Orders

Section 17(2) of the Family Law (Divorce) Act 1996 orders relate specifically to "retirement benefits".

In public sector type pension schemes, the retirement benefits "package" consists of a lump sum retirement gratuity, a retirement pension and a contingent spouse's pension of 50 per cent of the scheme member's pension, payable on the death of that member. A pension adjustment order made in favour of the non-member spouse will

---

*John McCarthy, B.Sc. FIA, Actuary, is a pensions consultant with The Pensions Settlement Bureau and acts as an expert witness in family law cases

specify a relevant period and a relevant percentage. Thus the order will effectively determine that the same proportion of each element of the "package" is to be earmarked for the benefit of the non-member spouse.

This causes a particular problem in relation to the spouse's pension payable on the death after retirement of the scheme member. Although this latter element is very much a contingent benefit, it is not defined as such in the legislation. This is a clear defect in the legislation which regularly causes problems in practical work. These problems are outlined in more detail in paragraph 2(c) of this chapter and by way of a Case Study in 4(e).

It is also noted that orders have been served on pension scheme trustees which specify a trivial relevant period and a trivial relevant percentage. Such orders have been made to utilise the "blocking order" provisions of section 17(26) of the Family Law (Divorce) Act 1996. In practice, trivial orders cause considerable problems for pension scheme trustees and there is a lobby from within the pensions industry to change the legislation. This aspect is discussed in more detail in paragraph 3 III of this chapter.

### (b) Contingent Benefits Orders

Orders under section 17(3) of the Family Law (Divorce) Act 1996 relate specifically to benefits which are payable on the contingency that the scheme member dies while a member of the pension scheme on which the order is served. Two areas of potential practical difficulty are worthy of note.

First, once a Court makes an order under the foregoing section, it does not appear to have the power under section 22 of the Family Law (Divorce) Act 1996 to vary the order in the event of a material change in circumstances. This appears to be an omission from the legislation, given that the Court has the power to vary section 17(2) orders (unless the original order contained a blocking provision pursuant to section 17(26).)

In practice, situations often occur where there are dependent children in the care of the non-member spouse and where maintenance is payable. It is possible to provide an actuarial estimate of the amount of death in service benefit which would currently be required to protect a given level of maintenance. However, the level of protection required to protect maintenance is likely to decrease over time; first because the cost of securing an income for the spouse decreases with the age of that spouse and secondly because the future period of dependency of the children reduces over time. I see no real reason why the legislation excludes contingent benefits orders from being varied in the future and I therefore suggest that this matter requires further consideration.

A further practical problem is that the legislation specifies that contingent benefits orders must be made at the same time as the decree or within 12 months thereafter. Bearing in mind that an order is served on the trustees of a specified pension scheme, it is possible (and it has happened in practice), that the member leaves the specified pension scheme and joins another scheme more than 12 months after the making of the decree. It would appear that the Court does not have the power to make an order, served on the trustees of the new scheme, which replaces the original protection for the non-member spouse. In my opinion, the legislation should be changed so that a further 12-month time limit applies in the event that a scheme member leaves a scheme upon which a section 17(3) order has been served.

### (c) Pension Preservation Orders

It is worthy of note that orders requiring pension scheme trustees not to regard the separation of the spouses as a ground for disqualifying any spouse's benefits which may otherwise have become payable, can only be made under section 13 of the Family Law Act 1995. There is no equivalent provision in the divorce legislation.

The above can give rise to a particular practical problem which is now occurring regularly in practice. Many divorces are by consent, on terms which are to be in accordance with a deed of separation made in the past. Such deeds often specify that the non-member spouse is to retain spouse's pension rights in full. In such a situation, the death in service benefit can be dealt with by way of a section 17(3) order, specifying that the contingent spouse's death in service pension is the designated benefit and also specifying a relevant percentage of 100 per cent. With regard to the contingent spouse's death after retirement pension, the Court can only deal with the benefit which has accrued to the date of the divorce. Hence it is not possible to obtain court orders on divorce which reflect a separation agreement provision to retain a spouse's pension rights in full. The only practical solution to this problem is to place an actuarial value on the loss of the spouse's rights on divorce and to reflect this value in the overall settlement terms for other assets.

## (d) Financial Compensation Orders

It appears that the intention of the legislation is to give the courts the power to require persons to effect or maintain life insurance policies so as to provide financial protection for divorced spouses in addition to, or in lieu of, similar protection provided by orders served on pension scheme trustees.

However, the legislation is considerably less precise in relation to financial compensation orders than in relation to pension scheme orders. In the case of the latter, orders are served on the trustees of the pension scheme and those trustees then have responsibilities to the non-member spouse under the Occupational Pension Schemes (Disclosure of Information) Regulations 1998 (S.I. No. 568 of 1998). For example, Trustees are required to provide regular information to the non-member spouse regarding the designated benefits and to inform that person, and the registrar or clerk of the court, if the member leaves service.

Where a financial compensation order is made, the legislation does not impose any obligations upon the insurance company whose policy is subject to the order. This could cause very serious problems if, for example, the policy lapses through non-payment of premiums and the insured spouse dies.

In my opinion, the lack of definition of the responsibilities of the insurer to the relevant persons and to the court is a serious defect in the legislation regarding financial compensation orders. It would therefore appear that the intended purpose of the financial compensation sections of the legislation is not being achieved. Amongst practitioners, a financial compensation order is generally regarded as being of much less value and quality to a beneficiary than orders served on pension schemes. This is because of the uncertainties surrounding the beneficiary of a financial compensation order's precise relationship with the insurance company. In my opinion, the legislation should be enhanced in this respect.

## 3. THE PENSIONS SETTLEMENT PROCESS — SOME PROBLEMS IN PRACTICE

In order to assess how the system for settling pension scheme issues is working in practice, a working party of the Society of Actuaries in Ireland has put forward the following criteria against which practical experience might be judged:

I.    That the parties to a family law action give full consideration to the relevant pension scheme implications in the light of appropriate information concerning the scheme benefits at issue.

II.   That orders served on trustees under the Family Law Acts are precisely defined and are capable of being implemented.

III.  That orders served on trustees under the Family Law Acts do not place unduly onerous additional administrative responsibilities upon those Trustees.

IV.   That orders made under the Family Law Acts do not increase the financial liabilities of the pension scheme concerned.

It is in the context of the above criteria, and in the light of actual cases in which I have been professionally involved, that I comment upon the practical issues.

## I (a) Availability of Appropriate Information

Sections 17(24) of the Family Law (Divorce) Act 1996 make specific reference to information rights under section 54 of the Pensions Act 1990 in situations where family law proceedings have been instituted. Section 54 of the Pensions Act was amended recently, by section 28 of the Social Welfare Act 1998, to make it clear that a non-member spouse does not have a right to obtain specific information about the member's benefits from the scheme's trustees. Thus trustees will not release appropriate information to an applicant for a pension adjustment order without first obtaining the consent of the scheme member. This causes delays, additional costs and has resulted in applications coming before the Court where, in my opinion, all of the relevant facts about the benefits at issue have not been suitably appraised in advance.

Before the Pensions Act was amended, section 54 could have been interpreted such that a non-member spouse in a family law action had rights which "may accrue", and therefore that scheme trustees were obliged by that section to provide appropriate information. In practice, the pensions industry was concerned about confidentiality and, notwithstanding section 17(24) in the Family Law (Divorce) Act 1996, scheme trustees were advised, by the Irish Association of Pension Funds and by Guidance Notes issued by the Pensions Board, not to release information to non-member spouses without the prior consent of the scheme member or a Court order under section 17(25) of the Family Law (Divorce) Act 1996.

In my opinion, subsection (24) of the 1996 Act was inserted for the purpose of ensuring that appropriate information about pension scheme benefits is made available to both parties in a family law action, once proceedings have been instituted. In practice, a lobby from within the pensions industry has succeeded in frustrating this intention by having section 54 of the Pensions Act amended to the effect that, under no interpretation of the amended Section, does a non-member spouse have any rights to pension scheme information from scheme trustees.

## I (b) Quality of the Information Provided

In practice most trustees, on receipt of a request for information from a solicitor advising a non-member spouse, have only answered the specific questions posed. If these questions are not sufficiently comprehensive, it can lead to inadequate assessments of the situation and potentially inappropriate orders being made.

I would conclude from I(a) and I(b) above that objective I is not being achieved in practice. In my experience and opinion, appropriate information has not been made available to both parties in advance of Court hearings and applications have often come before the Court based upon outdated and incomplete information about the benefits at issue. Since scheme trustees undoubtedly have all of the necessary information at their disposal, I consider that their obligations to make such information available in family law situations should be much more rigorously defined.

## II The Format and Drafting of Pension Adjustment Orders

There are several references in the legislation to "relevant guidelines". In this regard, the Pensions Board has published a comprehensive set of Guidance Notes which cover not only those sections of the Acts where guidelines are mentioned, but also the practical aspects of giving effect to pension adjustment orders. One such Guidance Note (G.N.) is G.N. 79, which covers the information scheme trustees need to give effect to orders under the Family Law Acts. In practice, orders have been made which do not contain all of the information specified in G.N. 79. It may therefore be difficult, or even impossible, for scheme trustees to operate an order in accordance with the intentions of the Court. Orders have also been made which do not appropriately define the benefits which are subject to the order, and which may therefore be ambiguous. I have even seen orders which do not make reference to the appropriate section of the Act under which they are made and which may therefore be of questionable legality.

In my opinion, the most likely situations in which incomplete orders can arise is in consent order situations, where the orders are often drafted in haste following "steps of the Court" negotiations on the day of the scheduled hearing. I would respectfully suggest that the whole subject of the drafting of Family Law Act orders to agreed standards is one which is worthy of more detailed consideration within the legal profession.

### III Pension Adjustment Orders for "Trivial" Amounts of Retirement Benefits

Reference has already been made in section 2(a) of this chapter to orders for trivial amounts of retirement benefits, so as to utilise the "blocking order" provisions of section 17(26) of the Family Law (Divorce) Act 1996. Thus orders have been drafted which specify, for example, a relevant period of one day and a relevant percentage of 0.1 per cent.

There are many examples in practice where the parties to a divorce agree not to make any claim over the pension rights of the other at any time in the future. A typical example is where both are in pensionable employment. In the opinion of the practitioners seeking trivial orders, the only way of giving effect to the agreement of the parties not to seek pension adjustment orders in the future is to make a trivial order now with an accompanying "blocking order".

However, it should be noted that trivial orders cause additional administrative requirements for pension scheme trustees. Even though the amount of benefit to which the non-member spouse is entitled is effectively zero, the trustees must still comply with the Pensions Act 1990 and the Occupational Pension Schemes (Disclosure of Information) Regulations 1998 in relation to this "benefit". Thus trivial orders can give rise to the somewhat ludicrous situation where a person must receive an annual benefits statement, confirming that the benefit is still effectively zero, an annual report relating to the operation of the scheme from which they derive no benefits, etc.

In my opinion, this matter requires discussion within the legal profession. If it is considered valid to make orders specifying a relevant percentage of zero, the pensions industry could apply to the authorities for an exemption from the regulatory requirements in relation to zero orders. Alternatively, and more preferably, the legislation could be amended to give Courts the power to make orders which extinguish all rights to apply for pension adjustment orders in the future.

## IV Interaction Between Retirement and Contingent Benefits Orders

Where a Court decides to grant both a retirement benefits order and a contingent benefits order, it is possible that the combination of the two orders could increase the financial liabilities of the pension scheme concerned. I submit that this is not the intention of the legislation and therefore that extra care is required.

As an example of the above problem, consider a defined contribution scheme under which the current value of retirement assets is £100,000 and within which the death in service benefit is defined as £200,000. In such circumstances, it would be usual for the trustees to purchase £100,000 of life cover on the scheme member to provide the total death in service cover (*i.e.* the £200,000 payable on death is payable; £100,000 from the retirement fund and £100,000 from the life insurance).

If a Court made a retirement benefits order in the amount of 50 per cent of retirement assets (current value £50,000) and a contingent benefits order specifying 100 per cent of the defined contingent death in service benefit (current amount £200,000), the total prescribed payment on the death of the scheme member would be £250,000. This latter amount would exceed the financial resources of the scheme. In order to avoid such a problem, the contingent death in service benefit should be described in the order such as to include the value of the designated retirement assets, where the scheme is of the type which makes it appropriate to make this distinction.

## 4. THE PENSIONS SETTLEMENT PROCESS — PRACTICAL ISSUES AND CASE STUDIES

### A. Retirement Benefits — Why a Pension Adjustment Order?

*(a) Long Term Security of Maintenance — Case Study I*

John is a senior manager for an international computer company. He earns a substantial salary, receives productivity bonuses and is entitled to participate in his company's share option scheme. He is also a member of his company's staff pension scheme.

Mary gave up her position as a junior secretary soon after marriage to look after the children. Now that the four children are virtually grown up, she has secured some part-time, non-pensionable work as a sales assistant in a local ladies fashion shop.

A preliminary assessment of the situation would conclude that this case is "all about maintenance". Mary will need some form of financial support from John for the rest of her life, because she has limited income-earning capacity and has not accrued any pension rights. John can certainly afford to pay a reasonable amount of maintenance from within his current employment. However, once he retires, his pension will only be a fraction of his pre-retirement earnings. Thus it is virtually certain that, whatever level of maintenance is agreed now, John will apply for a downward variation in maintenance after he retires, on the grounds of a material change in circumstances.

A degree of long-term financial security can be achieved for Mary by way of a pension adjustment order over a percentage of the 20 years of pensionable service which has accrued to John to date. While this is unlikely to guarantee Mary a retirement income equal to maintenance at the current level, she will at least "know where she stands" after John retires and can plan her finances accordingly. Furthermore, since John's pension scheme is of the "defined benefit, final salary" type, the benefit which is earmarked for Mary under the terms of a pension adjustment order, will increase in the future in line with John's pensionable salary.

*(b) A Degree of Equity Between Respective Pension Rights — Case Study II*

Frank and Nuala are both teachers. Nuala took a career break for 12 years to raise three children. This means that Frank now has 24 years of accrued pensionable service while Nuala only has 12. Furthermore, Frank is at a higher point on the teachers' salary scale because his service has been unbroken. In pension scheme terms, Nuala feels that she has borne the full cost of rearing the family. The solution is for her to obtain a pension adjustment order which specifies a relevant period of the 12 years of her career break and a relevant percentage of 50 per cent.

*(c) Compensation — Case Study III*

Jim operates a successful haulage company with 30 vehicles on the road. This business was built from scratch, initially with one vehicle which Jim drove himself. In the early days, Catherine helped out by taking orders, typing invoices, doing the accounts etc. Some years ago, Jim's accountant advised him to set up a defined contribution pension scheme for himself, so as to shelter some of the company's profits from tax.

Catherine now manages a flower shop and does not require substantial financial support from Jim. However she feels very aggrieved that she has not derived an appropriate reward from the success of Jim's company, given that she made a significant contribution towards building up that company in its early years.

One way of securing some appropriate compensation for Catherine is by way of a pension adjustment order over a percentage of the retirement fund which has accumulated in Jim's name. Since this fund has grown with investment performance to a substantial six figure sum, Catherine can acquire a tangible asset for her long term benefit from the business she helped to build.

*(d) Negotiation — Case Study IV*

Seamus is a Garda Sergeant and Marie is a nurse. Each is a member of the public service Superannuation Scheme appli-

cable to their employment. Their salaries are similar and
Seamus has accrued 24 years of pensionable service while
Marie has accrued 21 years. Marie is very attached to the
family home but cannot afford to buy out Seamus' 50 per
cent share.

At first glance, this would not appear to be a case for a
pension adjustment order, because both parties have accrued
rertirement benefits in their own right. However, an actuarial assessment of the accrued pension rights of the parties
revealed that the benefits standing to the credit of Seamus
are substantially more valuable than Marie's. Gardaí can re-
tire with full benefits after 30 years' service, at which point
Seamus will be aged 51. Marie can only qualify for full benefits if she completes 40 years' service by age 65. Thus
Seamus' accrued pension rights have a current value of
£210,000 while Marie's are only worth £90,000.

Marie therefore has a valid negotiating position regarding settlement terms for the family home. In lieu of making a
claim over Seamus' accrued pension rights, Marie was able
to reduce substantially Seamus' claim over 50% of the family home.

### (e) The Spouse's Death After Retirement Problem — Case Study V

Tom and Áine separated five years ago by way of an amica-
bly negotiated deed of separation. Under the terms of the
deed it was agreed that Aine was to retain her spouse's pension rights in full. They both now wish to obtain a divorce,
on settlement terms which reflect the deed of separation. Tom
recently retired at age 56 on ill-health grounds from the Local Government Officers Superannuation Scheme. His pension and lump sum are calculated on the basis of his
completed service of 23 years plus a further seven years'
notional service under the terms of the ill-health provisions
of the Superannuation Scheme.

Tom's pensionable salary at retirement was £27,000 per
annum. The breakdown of his retirement benefits was as follows:

| | |
|---|---|
| Retirement Gratuity | £30,375 |
| Retirement Pension | £10,125 p.a. |
| Spouse's Pension on Death | |
| After Retirement | £5,062 p.a |

In this example Aine was able to protect her spouse's pension rights by way of a section 17(2) order because all of the benefit had accrued prior to the date of the divorce.

However, in the more common situation, some spouse's rights will be lost on divorce. In the case of Aidan and Bernie, for example, Aidan had only accrued 20 years of retirement benefits to the date of divorce and he had another 20 years of potential membership of the Superannuation Scheme to go. In this case, it was only possible to protect 20 years worth of Bernie's spouse's pension rights. Following an actuarial assessment, the estimated current value of the potential loss to Bernie on divorce was £5,200, and this was factored into the settlement terms for other assets.

## B. Contingent Benefits — What Death in Service Cover is Required?

In simple terms, contingent benefits orders under section 17(3) of the 1996 Act are all about protection of maintenance. Since maintenance will obviously cease on the death of the providing spouse, the financially dependent spouse needs to ensure that there is adequate death benefit cover in place to secure a future income.

*(a) Pension Scheme Orders — Case Study VI*

Damien is a head of department in an insurance company. Under the terms of his company's pension scheme, the amounts which would be payable on his death are a lump sum of £100,000 and a spouse's pension of £6,250 per annum.

Damien currently pays maintenance to Sarah of £300 per week, made up of £150 per week for Sarah and £50 per week for each of the three children, currently aged 18, 16 and 14.

If Sarah is made the beneficiary of the spouse's death in service benefit by way of a contingent benefits order under section 17(3) of the 1996 Act, this would secure her maintenance protection of £120 per week. The lump sum cost of securing the remaining £30 per week is approximately £40,000. Hence it can be concluded that Sarah needs a contingent benefits order for her own protection in the amount of 40 per cent of Damien's lump sum death in service cover. In addition, it can be estimated that the lump sum which would be required to secure the children's maintenance while they remain dependent is currently £10,000 for the eldest child, £16,000 for the second eldest and £20,000 for the youngest.

The appropriate solution is therefore to make a contingent benefits order which specifies the following percentages of the contingent death in service lump sum to be payable to Sarah:

86% if all 3 children are dependent on Damien's death,
76% if the 2 youngest children are dependent on Damien's death,
60% if the youngest child is dependent on Damien's death, and
40% if none of the children are dependent on Damien's death.

### (b) Pension Scheme Order and Financial Compensation Order — Case Study VII

Cathal runs his own plumbing business on a self-employed basis. Over the years he has contributed to various personal pension policies. Under the terms of these policies, the payment on Cathal's death would be their value at the time of his death. Currently, the death benefit value of these policies is £50,000.

Cathal currently pays maintenance to Helen of £200 per week. The lump sum cost of securing an income at this level for Helen if maintenance were to cease would be £250,000 (Helen is 48 years of age).

Thus, even if a contingent benefits order in Helen's favour is made over 100% of the death in service benefits under Cathal's pension policies, there would still be a shortfall of £200,000 in maintenance protection cover. The cost of a term life insurance policy to age 65 on Cathal's life for a sum insured of £200,000 (he is a 50 year old non-smoker) would be £90 per month.

A satisfactory solution from Helen's viewpoint would therefore be a financial compensation order requiring Cathal to effect and maintain a life insurance policy for a sum insured of £200,000, in addition to obtaining a contingent benefits order over the death in service element of Cathal's pension policies.

## 5. CONCLUSION

There are undoubtedly some weaknesses in the current legislation and in some aspects of the pensions settlement process. Hopefully, these problems will be addressed in due course by the appropriate persons and bodies. Nevertheless, there is now an accumulating wealth of practical experience in negotiating and ruling on appropriate settlements. In real life, each case is different. What is required in everyday situations is an appreciation of the key issues and the expertise to engineer acceptable solutions.

# Index